PROHIBITION IN THE UPPER PENINSULA

BOOZE & BOOTLEGGERS ON THE BORDER

RUSSELL M. MAGNAGHI

AMERICAN PALATE

Published by American Palate
A Division of The History Press
Charleston, SC
www.historypress.net

First published 2017

Manufactured in the United States

ISBN 9781467119443

Library of Congress Control Number: 2016934533

Notice: The information in this book is true and complete to the best of our knowledge. It is offered without guarantee on the part of the author or The History Press. The author and The History Press disclaim all liability in connection with the use of this book.

Contents

Acknowledgements

Colleen Aho, Negaunee, Michigan
Irma Amichangelo, Iron Mountain, Michigan
Annie and Leon Anderson, Hurley, Wisconsin
Bruno and Tony Andriacchi, Ishpeming, Michigan
Robert R. Archibald, Gwinn, Michigan
Robert M. Bailey, Mackinac Island, Michigan
Tony Bausano, Calumet, Michigan
Bay Community College Library, Escanaba, Michigan
Ted Bays, Marquette, Michigan
Ted Bogdan, Marquette, Michigan
Carlo and Mary Caliaro, Hermansville, Michigan
Jenny M. Cappo, Baltic, Michigan
Jeanette and Doc Centanino, Calumet, Michigan
Central Upper Peninsula & University Archives, Northern Michigan University, Marquette
Sam Chetto, Negaunee, Michigan
Joseph F. Davey, Mackinac Island, Michigan
Jack Deo, Marquette, Michigan
Silvio De Paoli, Caspian, Michigan
Felix and Laura Dozzi, Princeton, Michigan
Otto Erspalmer, Hurley, Wisconsin
Finnish American Historical Archive and Museum, Finlandia University, Hancock, Michigan.

David S. Haynes, Marquette, Michigan
Susan K, Hurley, Wisconsin
Otto W. Lang, Mackinac Island, Michigan
Jason Lund, Calumet, Michigan
Mackinac Island State Park Commission, Mackinaw City, Michigan
Ed Mantila, L'Anse, Michigan
Patti Masspa, Mackinac Island, Michigan
Joseph Meiskens, Marquette, Michigan
Joseph Meni, Princeton, Michigan
Michigan Technological University Archives, Houghton, Michigan
Carl Pellonpää, Ishpeming, Michigan
Morton H. Pero, Mackinac Island, Michigan
Peter White Public Library, Marquette, Michigan
Herbert E. Pfeiffman, Mackinac Island, Michigan
Frank St. Onge, North Lake, Michigan
James Shefchik, Marquette, Michigan
David Spelgatti, Ishpeming, Michigan
State Library of Michigan, Lansing, Michigan
Fred Stonehouse, Marquette, Michigan
Philip K. Truscott, Mackinac Island, Michigan
Virginia Van Linden, L'Anse, Michigan
Frank and Steve Verbanac, L'Anse, Michigan

Introduction

Prohibition entered the Upper Peninsula of Michigan in 1918. This forest-covered land tucked away in the border recesses of the north is bounded by Canada and three Great Lakes—Superior, Huron and Michigan—and separated from the Lower Peninsula of Michigan by the Straits of Mackinac. It is the size of New England minus Maine. It was a sparsely populated area where booze could be produced in the acres of forest or transported from Canada along serpentine waterways with miles of hidden landing places beyond the reach of the police and Federal Prohibition Enforcement agents. As its history shows, the region interacts vitally with the history of the United States. But the Prohibition story of the UP is a little-known or chronicled part of that larger story.

This border region was settled by Anglo-Saxon Protestants, many of whom were temperance folk. As the region developed, large numbers of immigrant Catholics accustomed to making and drinking wine and beer moved in. There would be a built-in struggle between these two opposing cultures.

Prohibition and problems with alcoholic beverages went back to the late 1600s, when the French and then the British introduced the Native Americans to brandy and rum as part of the fur trade. From the beginning, there were missionaries and military commanders who were horrified at the results of native drunkenness and did what they could to limit the trade in brandy and rum. It took nearly three hundred years—until May 1918—for the dream of temperance workers to come true when state prohibition went into effect.

This new cultural dictate imposed by the federal government and religious leaders came as a shock to the thousands of immigrants who grew up around the role of alcohol in their lives. Given the nature of this border region, the story will include the role played by Ontario bootleggers and also the role played by gangsters in Hurley, Wisconsin, the sin city across the Montreal River from Ironwood, two towns whose histories were intertwined. This is not a story of fancy speakeasies but one of Yoopers who successfully continued the use of alcohol despite the unpopular law.

The story of Prohibition in the Upper Peninsula has never been told in its entirety. Sensational stories emerged in newspapers, but few of these stories were complete in their telling. The story actually remains in the minds and hearts of individuals and those of the era, from 1918 to 1933, but they are all but gone. Many of these memories remain with relatives, oral interviews and newspaper accounts. Newspapers, probably the best source of detailed information, have been made extremely useful with the development of electronic indexing. Without this service, much of this story could not have been told. Other scattered sources consist of government records—local, state and national—especially arrest and court records, Coast Guard records and consular reports located in the National Archives in Washington, D.C., and in the Federal Records Center in Chicago. As is obvious, these isolated and scattered records demand a lot of digging, except in this case, the needle was quickly found in the documentary haystack.

The Prohibition era provided two stories of American society. One was the Roaring Twenties, when American manners and mores changed and men and women were liberated. This was the Jazz Age, with its dances, clothing, radios and photograph records playing the latest music while movies depicted a dream world. It was a time of fun and excitement as speakeasies thrived, and a knock on the door provided entry, illicit whiskey and a good time. However, there was a dark side to the era that was devastating to the American moral character. Because of the Eighteenth Amendment, anyone taking an illicit drink was a violator. Stills dotted the countryside as Whiskey Sixes and speedboats carried liquor across the region to urban centers. Gangsters and accompanying violence ruled the day, and the police never knew what awaited them when they approached a car or dwelling. "Dance hall" became a euphemism for brothel. All of these and other elements are part of the social history of the Upper Peninsula, told here in depth for the first time.

The History Press continues to publish titles that most presses would ignore. Because of this focus this monograph was researched and written, for which the reader and future generations can be thankful.

1
Awash in Liquor

The Upper Peninsula has a unique history from its earliest days in terms of the use of alcohol. The French who arrived in the mid-seventeenth century brought with them the fur trade, abetted by a trade in brandy. From their early arrival, the Jesuit missionaries saw the deadly effects of alcohol on the native population and railed against it. One of the first was Father Paul Le Jeune, SJ, who in 1632 at Quebec wrote of the destruction and depopulation of the Indians and noted that some Indians pleaded for an end to the trade in brandy. It was pointed out to the Jesuits that, once drunk, Indians "had an irrefutable excuse for whatever violence and destruction they committed." In a spree, their villages became "veritable images of hell" with the drunken Indians burning cabins, tearing ears and noses from the face and killing their opponents. The captains and elders could not stop them, and those seeking safety fled into the woods. The missionary stayed with his home and church and waited until the furor ended. Brandy debauched the very people that the missionary was there to convert and civilize. Also, there was the concern for the safety of the French settlers when Indians went on an alcoholic spree.

The first real prohibitionist in the UP was the Jesuit Étienne Carheil, stationed at St. Ignace. He wrote an extensive report to the governor about conditions at Mission St. Ignace in late August 1702. First, he attacked the "infamous and baleful trade in brandy" that led to acts of brutality and violence, contempt and insult. He noted that if Louis XIV knew of these conditions, he would immediately forbid the trade. Second, he highlighted what amounted to prostitution with the soldiers keeping Indian women for their pleasure and monetary reward. Third, widespread gambling among the soldiers and fur traders set a terrible example and scandal for the Indians. Carheil wanted to see the total prohibition of brandy trade. This earnest Jesuit was despised and hated by the fur traders and by Fort Pontchartrain d'Étroit commander, and later Louisiana governor, Antoine Cadillac for his stance. However, the issue was never settled because officials were bribed and the hard economic reality of the times. If the French prohibited brandy to the Indians, they would trade with the English for rum and as the French traders told the Jesuits, "Do you want Catholic Indians drinking brandy or Protestant Indians drinking rum?"

Some Indians, horrified at the effects of alcohol consumed by their people, called for an end to the trade in brandy that they considered poison and "took away our senses and cause us untimely death." Other Indians pointed out the physical destruction involved, the loss of finances to trade for useful goods and the destruction of family life. Time and again Indians pleaded with the French to prohibit the brandy trade. Many of the arguments by both the missionaries and Indians are similar to those of the twentieth-century prohibitionists.

The French and Indian War, which pitted the French and their Indian allies against the British, ended in 1761. The French lost and were removed from North America. Now the English had total control of the fur trade and Indian affairs. In May 1761, British captain Donald Campbell called for a prohibition of rum to the Indians because of its destructive effects on them. Soon after, General Jeffery Amherst called for the total prohibition of rum to the Indians throughout British North America because of "the many evils that daily arose from allowing it to be sold to the Indians." Over the years, numerous incidents saw traders killed because they refused to trade rum to the Indians. Again we read stories of Indians in 1773 calling for a prohibition of rum because they saw more young men dying from rum than lost in warfare.

Nevertheless, outcast traders and vagabonds continued to introduce rum into the Great Lakes region. It was concluded that a police force would be needed to control the import of rum, which was impractical and costly. There was also the problem of Indians traveling, as they had in the French era, to Montreal and now to Albany and to obtain brandy or rum.

The British soldiers at Fort Michilimackinac had as their principal amusement drinking. Accounts tell of men and a trader who provided watered-down rum to the men and officers, who would have all-night parties consuming wine punch. A few of them became violent and belligerent and ended up breaking into residences, raping wives and severely beating the husbands when they tried to intervene. Fortunately, this activity involved a minority of individuals.

Rum continued to be important on the western border. In 1781, there were 3,084 gallons in storage at Fort Mackinac. Rum, rather than currency, was used to pay soldiers working on projects at the fort. At one point, this got costly for the British, and in 1815 at Drummond Island in the eastern UP, they decided to substitute cheaper porter or a good wholesome beer in place of rum. Despite all of the concerns for the effects of alcohol on the Indians and some would say on the British, liquor flowed into the Great Lakes much as it would during national Prohibition some 160 years later for all the same reasons.

Was liquor produced in the Upper Peninsula? We know that the recipe for spruce beer was introduced by the French. Not only did spruce beer have a "kick" to it, but its high vitamin C content prevented scurvy. Scurvy, commonly associated with long sea voyages, regularly broke out in the North Country, especially during the winter, when fruit and other sources of vitamin C were scarce. Spruce beer was relatively simple to make with local ingredients: spruce tips, maple sugar or molasses and water. The product was a low-grade beer, but most Frenchmen turned to readily available brandy. The British army, especially under General Amherst, promoted making spruce beer in the field, and it was readily available at Fort Mackinac. Alcoholic beverages were not that difficult to make locally, needing only fruit or potatoes, fermentation and then distillation. Little is written of this activity, as imported alcohol was readily available.

Prior to the War of 1812, a distillery—the first known in the Upper Peninsula—was opened on Mackinac Island. By the time of the war, it had been abandoned and was a place of refuge when the British invaded the island.

2

Struggle for State Prohibition

Throughout the nineteenth-century, alcohol abuse among the British and American soldiers stationed at Fort Mackinac was a major problem. The British army stationed there from 1812 to 1815 consisted of mostly illiterate enlisted men who could not gamble due to regulations and turned to alcohol. Liquor was a major problem for the U.S. Army stationed at the fort, and drunkenness was the major offense for being court-martialed. There was little that military authorities could do with the civilian saloonkeepers. In 1889, they opened a beer bar in the fort with the idea of keeping the men away from the hard liquor in the village.

Despite congressional and executive regulations and orders, liquor continued to flow into the Great Lakes region, and the Indians were debauched and degraded by firewater. In 1832, some 8,776 gallons of liquor landed at Mackinac Island. Although John Jacob Astor, head of the American Fur Company (AFC), tried to convince the Indians that they would be more productive without liquor, they did not listen. The old story arose—if AFC did not provide liquor, there were British sources.

Mackinac Island was the entrepôt of the fur trade and a social center. With the return of traders, the celebrating included banquets and dances until dawn and plenty of rum. Drunkenness, brawling and frequent murders were part of life.

The effects of alcohol on the native population scandalized the Catholic and Protestant missionaries arriving in the early nineteenth century. Baptist missionary Abel Bingham settled at Sault Ste. Marie in October 1828.

Liquor was plentiful, and intemperance was a common vice among the soldiers at Fort Brady, civilians and the Indians. As a result, he established the St. Mary's Temperance Society in May 1830, and most officers and soldiers, as well as fur traders, became members. Even the fort sutler, John Hulbert, who had been selling twenty pints of whiskey a day, took the pledge and lost revenue.

In the summer of 1835, Dr. Chandler Gilman, a New York City physician on a vacation to Lake Superior's Pictured Rocks, stopped at Sault Ste. Marie. He was appalled at the alcoholism among the Native American population—"slaves to rum," as he described them.

The Methodist missionaries worked in the Upper Peninsula and fought intemperance. One of these was Reverend John Pitzel, who worked unceasingly to end the liquor trade and Indian consumption of alcohol. At the same time, in the 1840s and 1850s, the Catholic missionary Frederic Baraga promoted temperance and had Catholics take a pledge. The Mormon leader on Beaver Island, James Strang, protested against the destructive adulterated whiskey trade to the Indians by fishermen and traders from Mackinac Island.

In the mid-1840s, the central and western Upper Peninsula was open to settlement with the development of the copper and iron ranges. Thousands of people settled the region, and an early group of these settlers were immigrants who loved their beer. In the summer of 1850, the first German brewery opened at Sault Ste. Marie. German breweries quickly multiplied so that every major community had one. The demand for beer and whiskey was readily met in stores, hotel bars, main street saloons and scrub taverns located throughout the mining districts. The men did rough work under dangerous conditions and felt that, at the end of the week, they should celebrate at the local saloon. These saloons were the poor man's equivalent to the social clubs to which wealthy Americans had access. The saloon was a social and fraternal headquarters where immigrants could feel at home. Mail could be delivered there, the latest local news spread and the salty food of the buffet encouraged beer to flow. Unions and fraternal organizations met in the saloon, which also developed political connections and provided tipplers with access to jobs. Every community, large and small, had its saloons, and many of them had breweries, as well. At the time, breweries could establish their own saloons or readily paid a prospective saloonkeeper to go into business, providing the entire bar equipment as long as the keeper served the financer's beer.

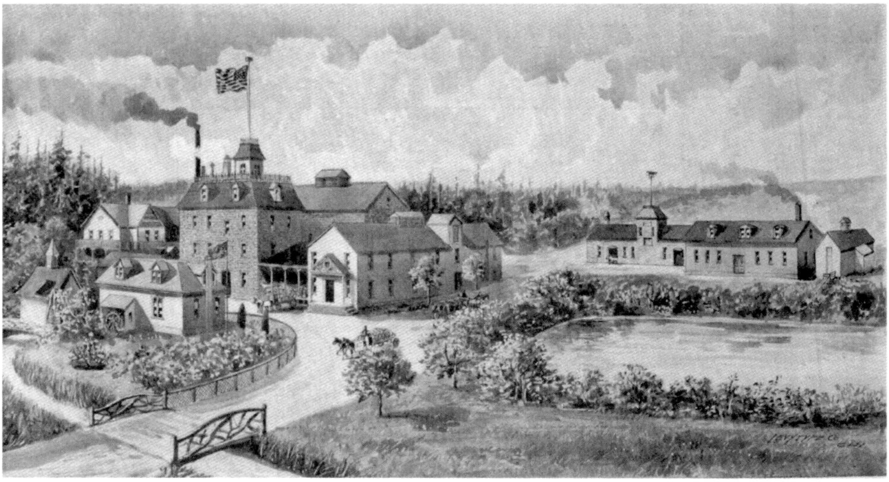

German immigrant and brewer Charles Meeske included a lake and beer garden on his property. *Courtesy of Superior View.*

The newspaper accounts provide insights into what was being sold in the saloons. Martin Vierling, who arrived in Marquette in 1868, developed a well-known establishment and in 1912 had "a large stock of the choicest Wines and Liquors" and, in particular, "the best brandys." He also had "ales and beers bottled, and in the wood." Rothschild & Bending was a liquor wholesaler covering a large area of Michigan, providing "all the leading and most popular Kentucky whiskies which they see either in bond or the finest Champagnes, Ports, Sherries, Moselles, Burgundies, Sauternes and other wines, both imported or from our own superior vineyards; Dubois, Lizet & Co., Martelle & domestic Cognacs; the best makes of rums; De Kuyper & other well known gins…and a fine line of imported cordials and liquors." One enterprising saloonkeeper in 1886 advertised in the *Marquette Mining Journal* that those who broke their temperance pledge were always welcome in his saloon.

In the center of the copper region, Calumet, with a population of 4,000 in 1877, had twenty-four saloons, or a saloon for every 166 residents. Similar figures can be tracked across the peninsula, with the iron-mining town of Republic's 1,000 people serviced by eight saloons. The use of alcohol was extensive, and many people like Father Baraga and others dreaded the Fourth of July, a day when liquor flowed and drunkenness was rampant and accompanied by fights.

In the eastern UP at Sault Ste. Marie and Mackinac Island, tourists replaced the fur traders. Hotels and restaurants provided tourists

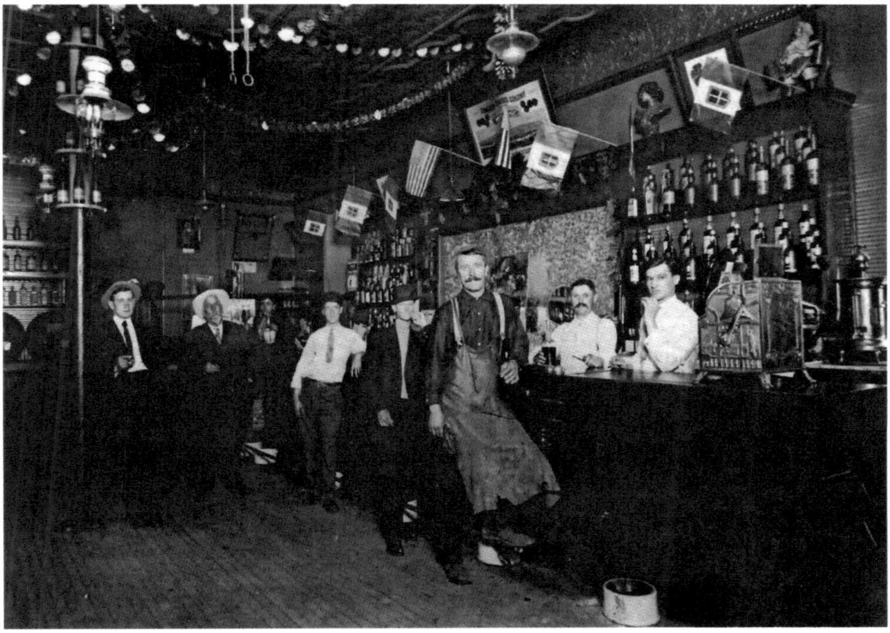

Bianchi's Saloon (circa 1905) was a typical saloon serving as a social club for Italian immigrants. *Courtesy of Marquette Regional History Center & R.M. Magnaghi.*

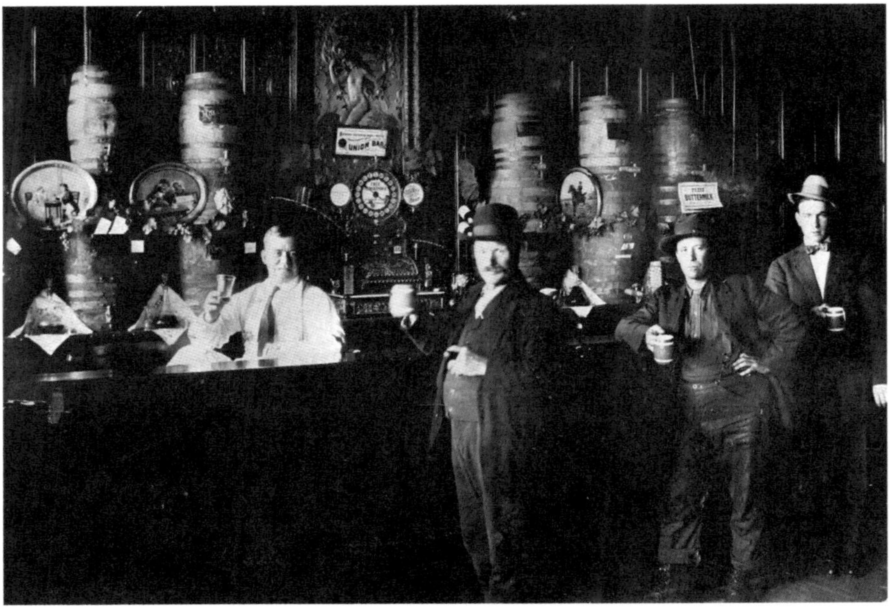

Early twentieth-century saloons like this one in Marquette served free lunches with salty foods to encourage beer drinking. *Courtesy of Superior View.*

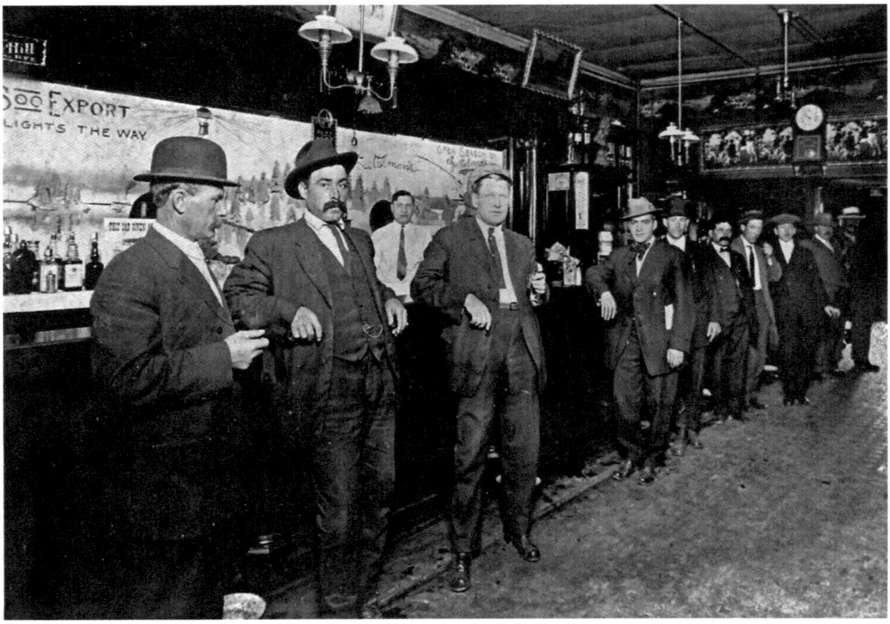

De Paul's Saloon in Sault Ste. Marie (1910) catered to soldiers from Fort Brady. *Courtesy of Marquette Regional History Center & R.M. Magnaghi.*

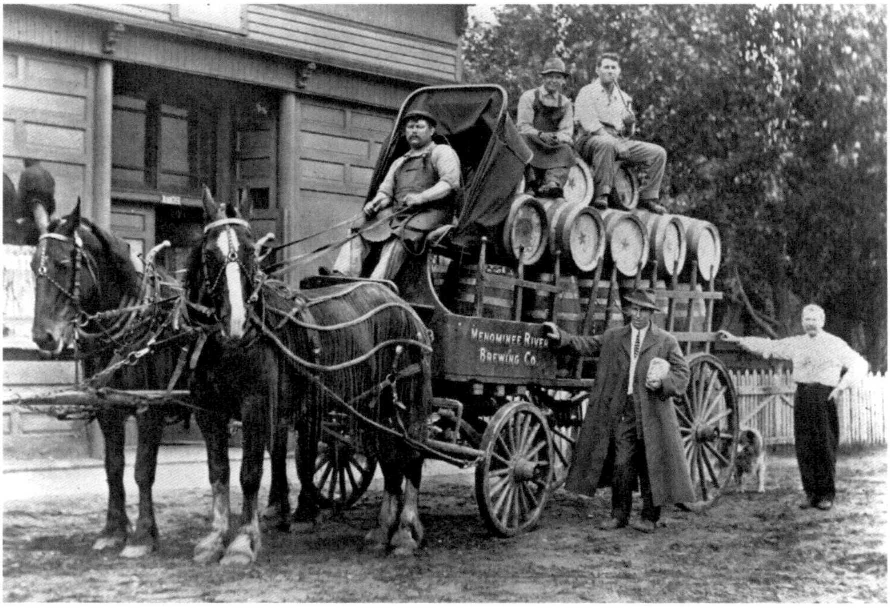

Such scenes ended with Prohibition. *Courtesy of Superior View.*

on this northwestern border fine food and liquid refreshment. In 1860, two "gin cocktail makers" were mixing drinks in local saloons. Mackinac Island continued its reputation as a social center, catering to affluent summer resorters.

The consumption of alcohol grew with the population and troubled many people. There were various groups that first promoted the temperance pledge, but others looked toward total prohibition of liquor because of its abuse. In the late nineteenth century, Finnish immigrants developed a very strong temperance movement throughout the Upper Peninsula. The mining and timber companies were also concerned about the overbearing consumption of liquor that was detrimental to the workforce. The timber companies did not allow liquor in their camps, and the mining companies prohibited liquor in their company towns. Laborers who were drunk on the job were fined, but some of the alcoholics paid the fine early to avoid a disruption to their drinking. To get around the regulations, lumberjacks headed for town as soon as their weekend started, and in mining communities, saloonkeepers found

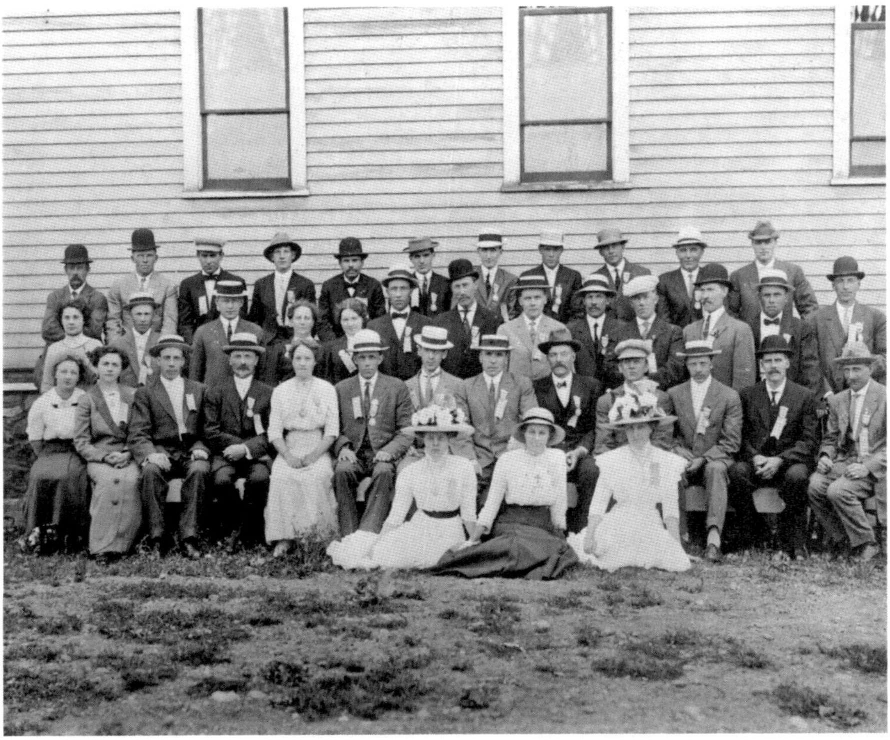

The Swedish-Finnish Temperance Society and similar societies were important promoters of Prohibition. *Courtesy of Superior View.*

ingenious ways to skirt the companies' rules. In Manistique, the Chicago Lumbering Company tried to keep the community dry, but saloonkeepers, in a classic example, got around the prohibition and opened the Flatiron Block and Alex Richard's saloons.

The negative aspect of liquor with its heavy drinking and drunkenness was well known to people in Michigan. Prior to statehood in 1837, reform-minded New England settlers arrived and brought with them the temperance concept. Earlier in 1826, the American Temperance Society

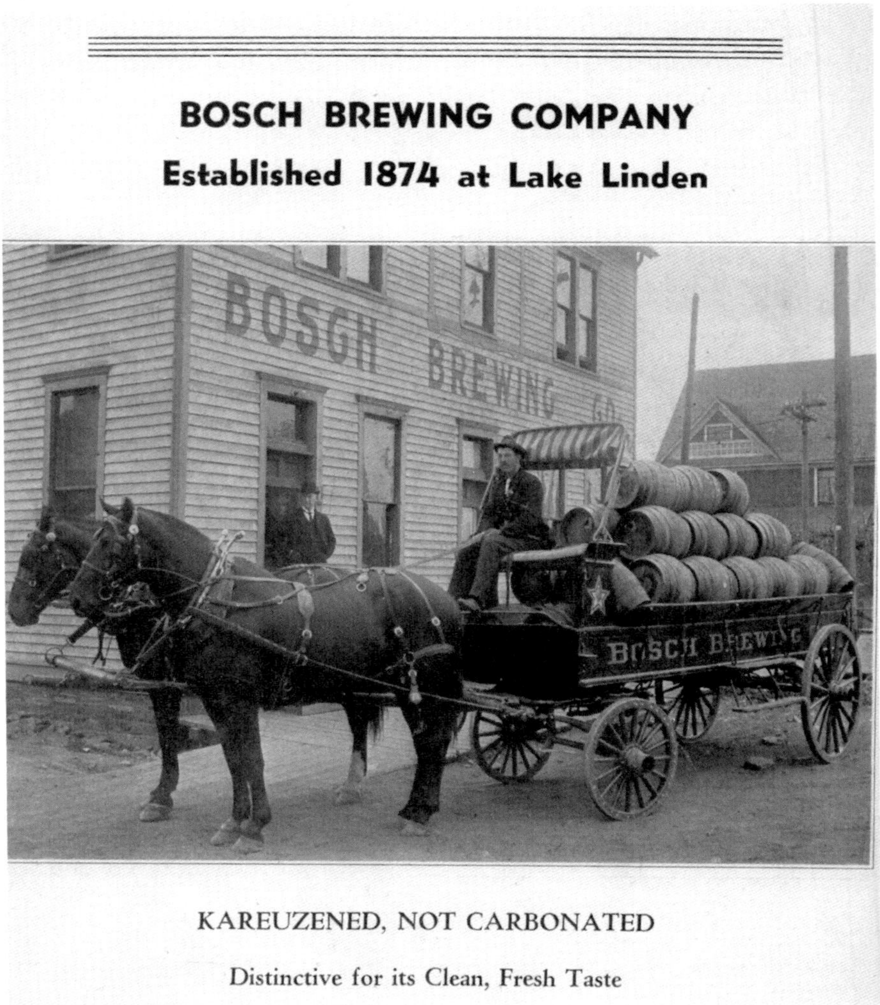

A Bosch delivery wagon. *Courtesy of Superior View.*

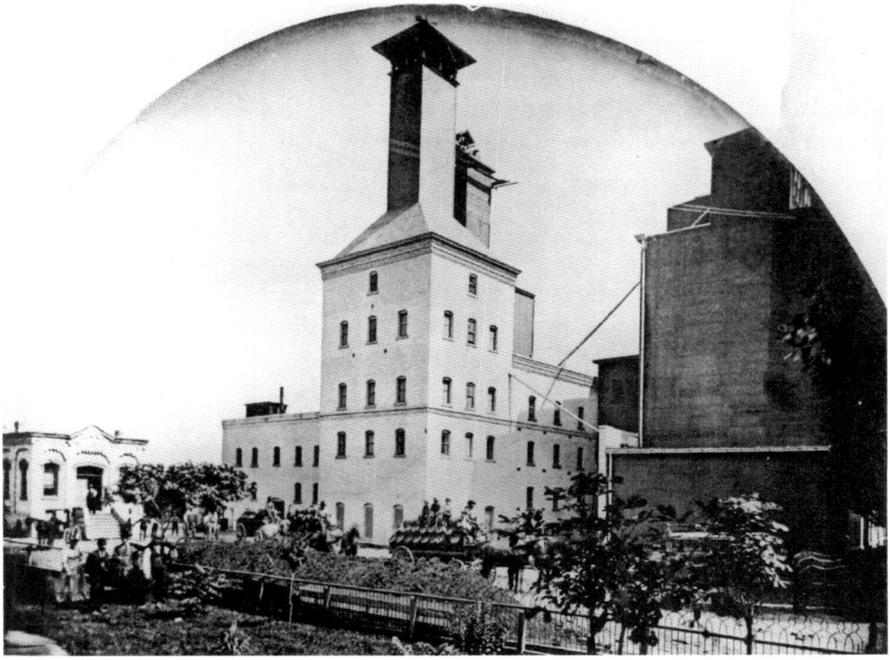

Leisen & Henes Malt House, Menominee, Michigan. *Courtesy of Superior View.*

was formed, followed by a Michigan society in 1833. Reverend Bingham had established the St. Mary's Temperance Society, the first in the UP, and in 1850 the Sons of Temperance at Sault Ste. Marie, also known as the Soo, continued the tradition.

First, it was felt that moral suasion and moderation should be followed, which brought few results. Next, they turned to abstinence from "ardent spirits." The only problem with this position was that ardent spirits were cheaper and more popular than the wine and beer that were promoted. Then, in the 1840, reformed drunkards took to the roads and promoted abstinence. One of these speakers was Augustus Littlejohn of Allegan, Michigan, who was an excellent orator with a tremendous stage presence. He connected temperance with religion and usually performed in churches. This union of temperance and religion would be the major force that brought about state and national Prohibition.

In 1851, the state of Maine's legislature passed a law that "prohibited the manufacture, sale, or keeping for sale of intoxicating liquors and set heavy penalties for violations." Michigan followed with a series of prohibition laws. In 1854, the state legislature passed a prohibition law that was declared invalid due to legal concerns. Then, a year later, a weak law, filled with loopholes, was passed that made the prohibition law unenforceable. This allowed 476 saloons, along with twenty-three breweries and six distilleries, to thrive in Detroit while the ineffective prohibition law remained on the books until 1875. This was followed by a watered-down law that closed saloons on Election Day, kept liquor from Native Americans and permitted "local option" votes in the counties.

The temperance forces wanted an end to saloons and got a constitutional amendment on the ballot for an April 4, 1887 vote to make Michigan a dry state. It failed but in a close vote: 184,305 against (wets) and 178,470 for (dries). The UP voted wet: 15,641 (71 percent) to 6,409 (29 percent). It would only be a matter of time before the prohibitionists would win in the state.

The saloons thrived, and the demand for beer was met by eighteen breweries, especially in the western UP, augmented by thousands of barrels arriving by rail from Milwaukee and St. Louis. In 1891 in the UP, there were 566 saloons; that number peaked in 1909 at 920.

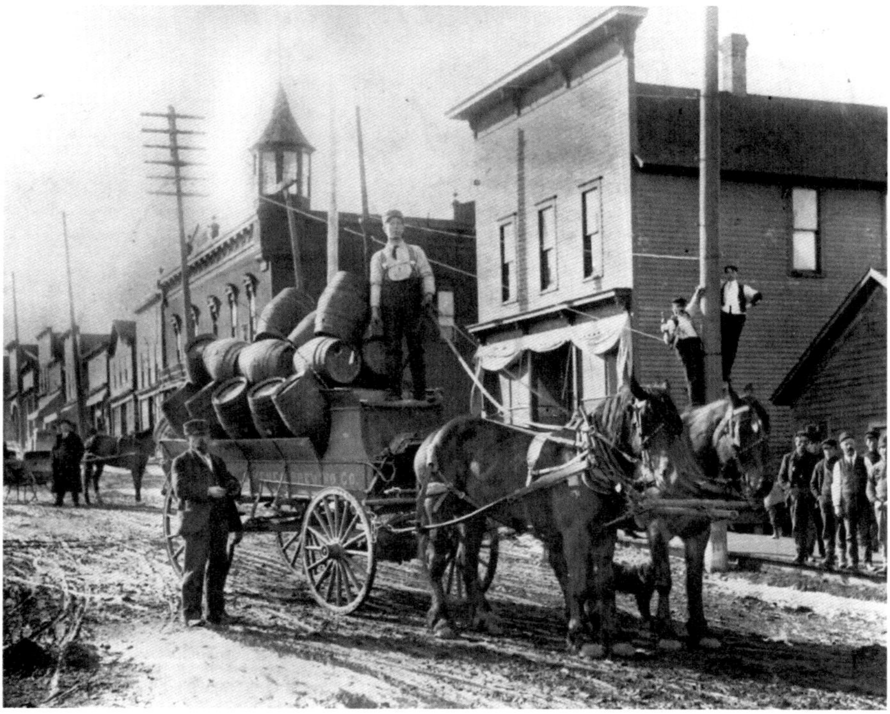

Leisen & Henes Brewing Company delivered in Crystal Falls. *Courtesy of Superior View.*

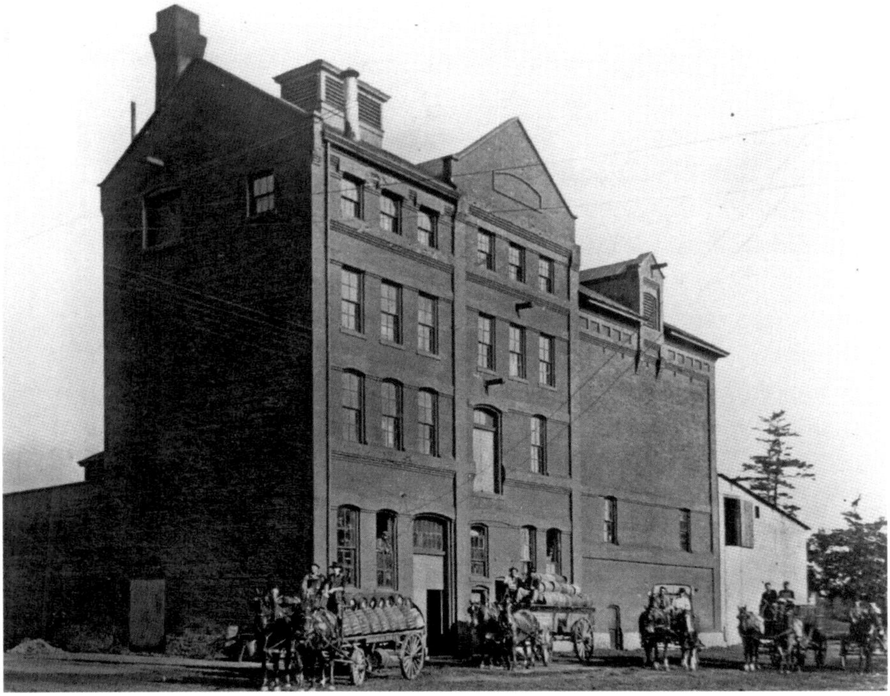

Escanaba Brewing Company. *Courtesy of Superior View.*

The UP author Robert Traver, aka John Voelker, in his work *Danny and the Boys* provides descriptions of saloons that flourished at the turn of the twentieth century and were what the temperance folk fought against. Charlie Jokinen, a Finnish immigrant who "possessed a constitutional allergy to all hard work, including iron-mining," owned Charlie's Place. His saloon was one of fourteen saloons on the town's Main Street, not to mention the many others on the side streets. On Saturday nights and on paydays, all of them were busy, for that was when hundreds of miners surged downtown, cashing their vouchers from the iron mines; paying bills; mingling with the lumberjacks and farmers; buying new boots, socks and heavy miners' underwear; and, to the dismay of the local temperance workers, "'sneakin' a few dollars on the ol' woman for a bloody drink or two!" Now moving into the Charlie's Place interior, Voelker continues his description of a typical early twentieth-century Upper Peninsula saloon:

> *Charlie's worn mahogany bar ran nearly half the depth of the long, high room. At the far end of the bar...stood the free-lunch counter, covered with*

cheesecloth against the droning flies. On the wall was a neatly printed sign: "Free lunch—25¢." A massive icebox flanked the counter. Beyond that was the partitioned, green-tabled poker tables, at the back of the saloon was a small kitchen and the "Sunday door," leading out to the alley in the rear. Over the entire establishment there hovered a delicious, stale, boozy smell—a subtle combination of stale beer, mustard, cold ham, old cheese, brine of pickled herring, spilt whisky, over-loaded spittoons, sweating men.

This was the type of saloon the ardent prohibitionists were trying to bring to an end.

Two points of view developed. Over the years, moderate groups formed to regulate the liquor business in all of its aspects. The National Model License League stressed the fact that, on a per capita basis, Americans drank twenty-three gallons of alcoholic beverages and that half the states in 1910 were dry. League president T.M. Gilmore pointed out that prohibition had little effect on state and county levels. The best way to regulate alcohol was through strict licensing and enforcement, not prohibition. This was also the position of members of the hierarchy of the Catholic Church.

On the other side were members of the Prohibition Party and the Woman's Christian Temperance Union, which were ineffective in bringing about statewide prohibition in Michigan. However, beginning in 1889, the state legislature passed a local option law, which allowed local communities to restrict liquor. Additional laws were built on this one so that by 1915, Michigan had a detailed set of laws relating "to the manufacture, sale and use of spirituous liquor." Licensing and location of saloons, sale of liquor to minors and veterans were among the items included in the series of laws. In 1909, free saloon lunches ended, but crackers and pretzels were still allowed.

Onto the scene came the Anti-Saloon League, which between 1893 and 1933 was a major political force in the United States. The league organized a branch in Michigan in 1896 and spread its ideals through lectures, publications, temperance meetings and, especially, churches. It supported, irrespective of political party, any candidate who promoted prohibition and worked on the local level.

The league was a power to be reckoned with, including in the UP. In 1906, at Lake Linden and Hubbell, elaborate prohibition rallies were held that included prominent speakers, budding politicians and street marches with local bands. At the twenty-first annual convention of the Michigan State Federation of Women's Clubs held in Lansing in November 1915, resolutions were passed endorsing statewide prohibition. The Calumet Women's Club

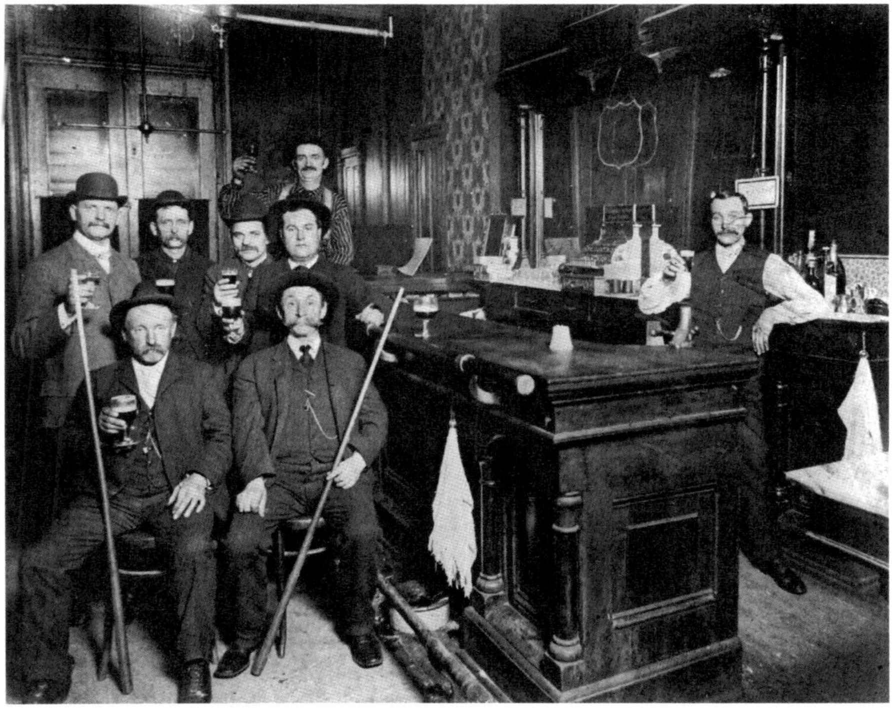

Beer and pool were a common part of saloon life. *Courtesy of Superior View.*

concurred with the resolution: "Whereas, we, 21,000 Michigan women, in convention assembled, believe that the organized legalized beverage drink traffic, carried on by breweries and saloons in our state and nation, have been proven with scientific accuracy and beyond a possibility of contradiction, to be the most deadly foe of our economic, industrial, civic, social, educational and religious institutions, the chief cause of the major portion of our crime, pauperism and political corruption." This could be a page from the Anti-Saloon League and shows the power of the prohibition movement as the November 1916 election approached.

The battle was unleashed by the Anti-Saloon League to get state prohibition passed. The wets considered the league composed of "zealots and fanatics." As the *Ironwood Times* wrote in retrospect in March 1930, the Anti-Saloon League was "converted into a vehicle for fanaticism, half truths, great campaign expenditures, highly paid lobbyists, and the most startling intolerance in the world's history."

In the months leading up to the election, dries invoked questionable "facts." Because World War I was raging, it was said that Germans had

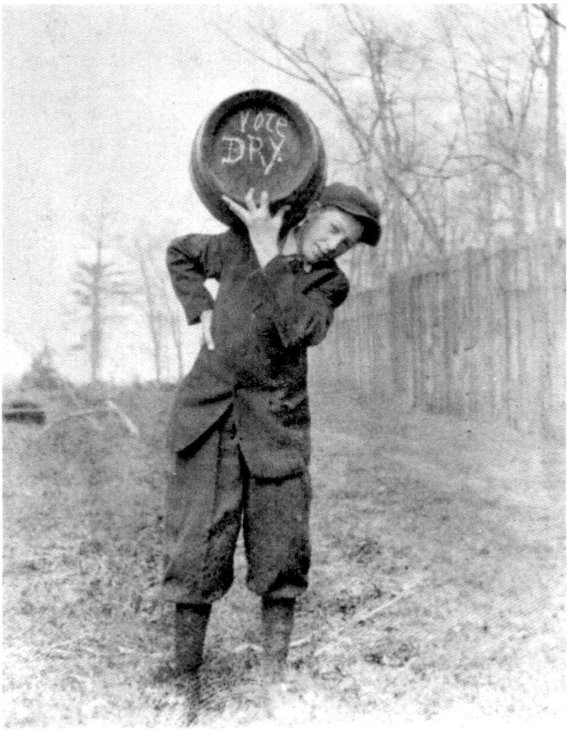

Left: Boy promoting "Vote Dry." *Courtesy of Superior View.*

Below: Mothers and children promoting Prohibition prior to the 1916 election. *Courtesy of History and Special Collections, Grand Rapids Public Library.*

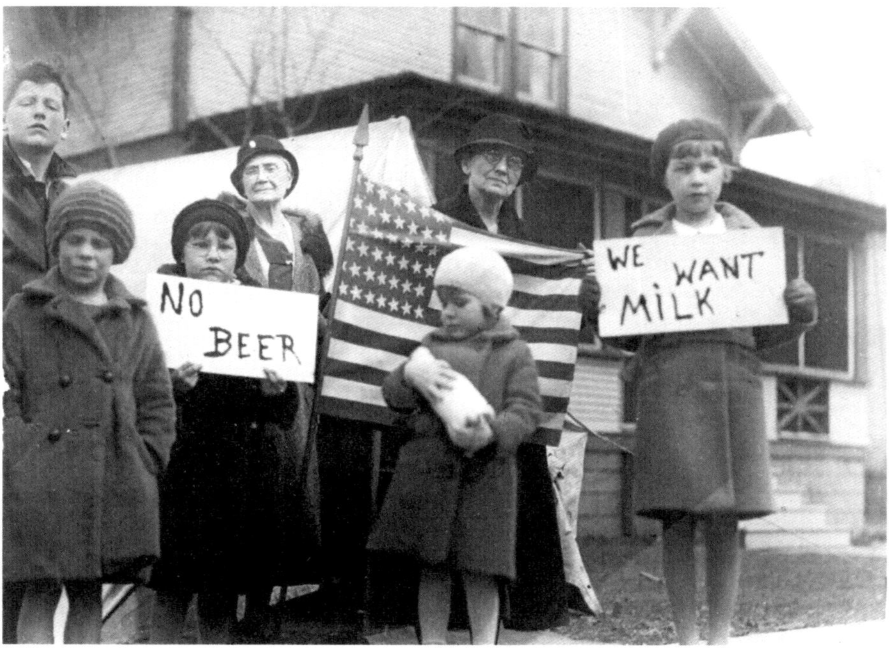

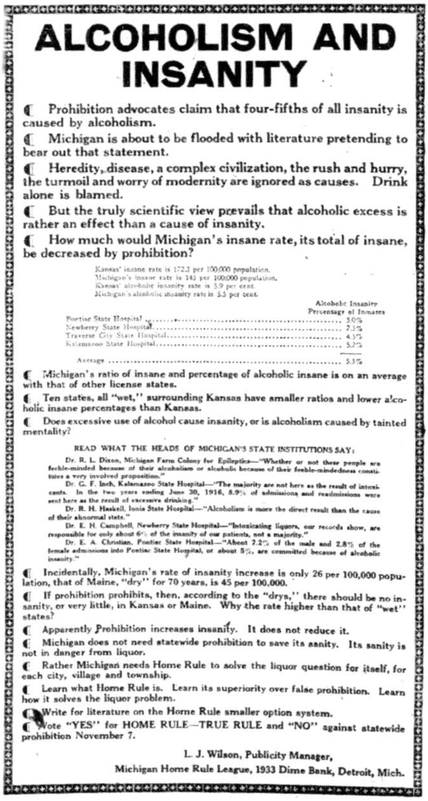

ALCOHOLISM AND INSANITY

Prohibition advocates claim that four-fifths of all insanity is caused by alcoholism.

Michigan is about to be flooded with literature pretending to bear out that statement.

Heredity, disease, a complex civilization, the rush and hurry, the turmoil and worry of modernity are ignored as causes. Drink alone is blamed.

But the truly scientific view prevails that alcoholic excess is rather an effect than a cause of insanity.

How much would Michigan's insane rate, its total of insane, be decreased by prohibition?

Kansas' insane rate is 172.3 per 100,000 population.
Michigan's insane rate is 145 per 100,000 population.
Kansas' alcoholic insanity rate is 5.9 per cent.
Michigan's alcoholic insanity rate is 5.5 per cent.

	Alcoholic Insanity Percentage of Inmates
Pontiac State Hospital	5.0%
Newberry State Hospital	7.3%
Traverse City State Hospital	4.5%
Kalamazoo State Hospital	5.2%
Average	5.5%

Michigan's ratio of insane and percentage of alcoholic insane is on an average with that of other license states.

Ten states, all "wet," surrounding Kansas have smaller ratios and lower alcoholic insane percentages than Kansas.

Does excessive use of alcohol cause insanity, or is alcoholism caused by tainted mentality?

READ WHAT THE HEADS OF MICHIGAN'S STATE INSTITUTIONS SAY:

Dr. R. L. Dixon, Michigan Farm Colony for Epileptics—"Whether or not these people are feeble-minded because of their alcoholism or alcoholic because of their feeble-mindedness constitutes a very involved proposition."

Dr. G. F. Inch, Kalamazoo State Hospital—"The majority are not here as the result of intoxicants. In the two years ending June 30, 1916, 8.9% of admissions and readmissions were sent here as the result of excessive drinking."

Dr. R. H. Haskell, Ionia State Hospital—"Alcoholism is more the direct result than the cause of their abnormal state."

Dr. E. H. Campbell, Newberry State Hospital—"Intoxicating liquors, our records show, are responsible for only about 6% of the insanity of our patients, not a majority."

Dr. E. A. Christian, Pontiac State Hospital—"About 7.2% of the male and 2.8% of the female admissions into Pontiac State Hospital, or about 5%, are committed because of alcoholic insanity."

Incidentally, Michigan's rate of insanity increase is only 26 per 100,000 population, that of Maine, "dry" for 70 years, is 45 per 100,000.

If prohibition prohibits, then, according to the "drys," there should be no insanity, or very little, in Kansas or Maine. Why the rate higher than that of "wet" states?

Apparently Prohibition increases insanity. It does not reduce it.

Michigan does not need statewide prohibition to save its sanity. Its sanity is not in danger from liquor.

Rather Michigan needs Home Rule to solve the liquor question for itself, for each city, village and township.

Learn what Home Rule is. Learn its superiority over false prohibition. Learn how it solves the liquor problem.

Write for literature on the Home Rule smaller option system.

Vote "YES" for HOME RULE—TRUE RULE and "NO" against statewide prohibition November 7.

L. J. Wilson, Publicity Manager,
Michigan Home Rule League, 1933 Dime Bank, Detroit, Mich.

Poster used to promote the Prohibition vote by the Anti-Saloon League. *Courtesy of History & Special Collections, Grand Rapids Public Library.*

been "brutalized" by beer. British chancellor of the exchequer David Lloyd-George was quoted, "We are fighting Germany and Austria and Drink, and so far as I can see the greatest of these deadly foes is drink." German immigrants and German Americans, especially brewers, were seen as trying to destroy America. The Anti-Saloon League made unsubstantiated statements—"The longer we are without it [the saloon] the less we miss it, the less anyone wants it back"—and threw around highly questionable figures: three thousand drunken men in Michigan had killed their wives, and seven hundred drunken mothers had strangled their babies.

The wets tried to use reason to support their position, as can be seen from the newspaper ads by the Michigan Home Rule League. The league pointed out that the Prohibitionist was labor's enemy: Prohibition would see the loss of fifty thousand jobs, put the laborer at the mercy of big business and throttle labor unions. There would also be the demise of $30 million in property closures. Bootleggers and blind pigs would fill the demand for liquor and millions would be lost in revenue for the government. The league concluded that the attack on liquor was just the start and that these reformers would go after theaters, dance halls and, ultimately, "a pipe-full of tobacco." Others promoted the healthy qualities of beer, which was referred to as "liquid bread."

Iron County was used as a model of the failure of prohibition. The county had gone dry in 1913, and within a year and a half, two-thirds of the people were voting wet due to the flood of blind pigs and bootleggers, the most lawlessness and drunkenness in the county's history, the farcical

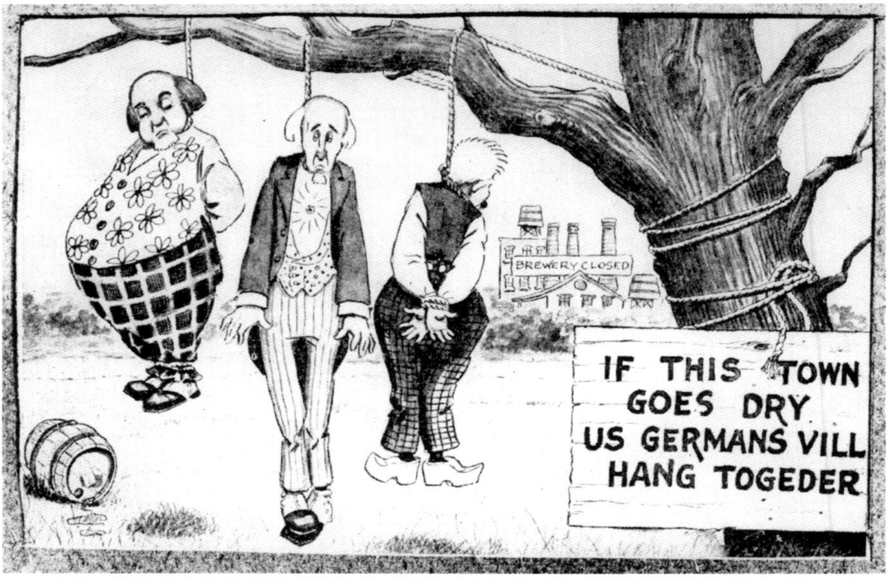

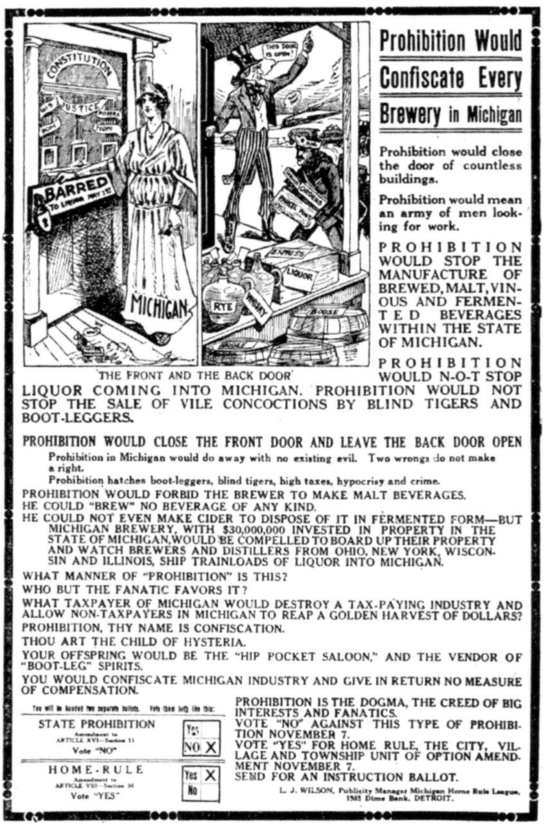

Above: Anti-German Prohibition cartoon. *Courtesy of History & Special Collections, Grand Rapids Public Library.*

Left: An advertisement against Prohibition. *Courtesy* of *History & Special Collections, Grand Rapids Public Library.*

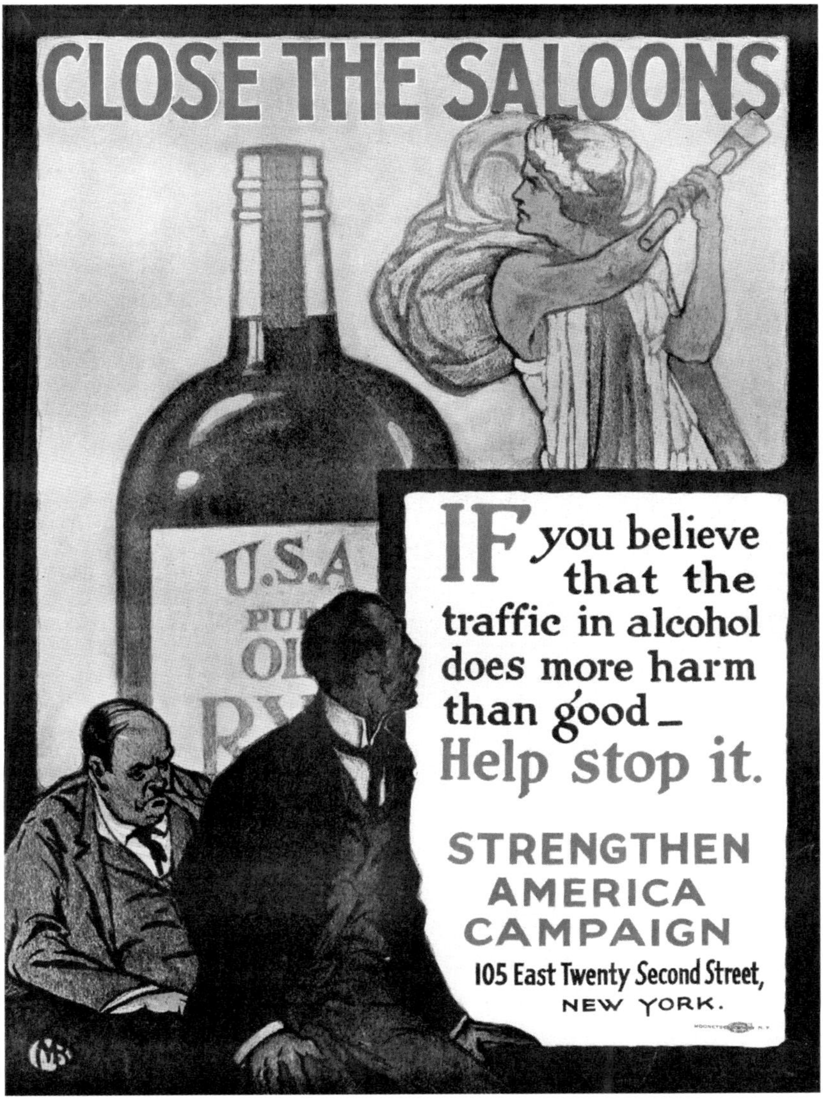

A poster from 1918. *Courtesy of Still Picture Unit National Archives.*

effort to enforce the law and the loss of $14,000 in taxes. This reasoning fell on deaf ears in the general public.

On November 7, 1916, the people of Michigan voted for the constitutional amendment—353,378 dry to 284,754 wet. The dries in the UP carried eleven of the fifteen counties, winning over 60 percent of the vote in six of the counties with large first- and second-generation immigrants. Some wets

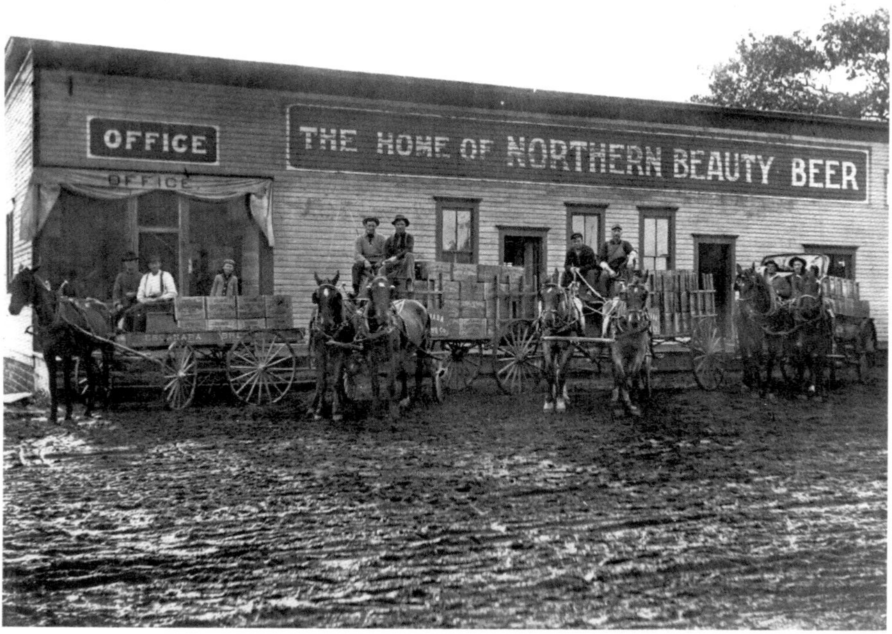

Beer delivery wagons left the streets with the advent of Prohibition. *Courtesy of Superior View.*

pointed out that the prohibition of liquor had been tried since colonial times and that it had never worked, but these advisements were too little, too late. Prohibition went into effect on May 1, 1918.

The Anti-Saloon League, under the leadership of Wayne Wheeler, moved ahead, and by January 16, 1919, the Eighteenth Amendment had been ratified and become the law of the land. The National Prohibition Act, commonly known as the Volstead Act, carried out the intent of the amendment. The bill was named after Andrew Volstead of Minnesota, chair of the House Judiciary Committee, who managed the legislation, but it was conceived and drafted by Wheeler. Years of struggle by the dries had born fruit. Would Americans give up imbibing for a constitutional amendment? Many said, "Look to Michigan to evade the law."

3

PROHIBITION, A REALITY

OR, HOW TO COPE

Banning liquor through the Eighteenth Amendment had the effect of making it more desirable. Old drinkers were not to be denied, and new drinkers found a new thrill possessing and partaking of illegal spirits. Law-abiding citizens were now lawbreakers when they bought and held a bottle of liquor or entered a speakeasy. The public was not to be denied.

The immediate effect of the start of state prohibition on May 1, 1918, was the closure of hundreds of saloons throughout the Upper Peninsula. For many owners, this was a jolt into reality—they were out of business. Some decided that it was time to retire. Others did not know where to turn now that their livelihoods were gone. For the immediate future, some of them opened soft drink parlors, lunch counters and billiard and pool establishments.

Across the UP, newspapers provide insights as to how these saloonkeepers dealt with the new era. In the copper country, the *Calumet News* provides some local examples: twenty-six-year bartender veteran A. Turcotte opened a pool hall, Antonio Giuglio followed with a billiard parlor, Charles McCann established a refreshment shop and John M. Foley opened a lunchroom. Martin Yaunch Sr. was nearing retirement after forty years in the saloon business, but his sons, Martin and William, turned the saloon room in the Haas Brewing Company's building into a billiard hall. One of the finest hotels in the UP, the Douglass House in Houghton, kept its bar open as a lounging room where refreshments were available.

Seeing that these soft drinking shops would become social centers, much as the saloons had been, communities licensed them. As time passed and problems arose, additions were made to the ordinances so that soft drink shops could not have screens or curtains on the windows, and they were forbidden to tolerate lewdness or immorality of any kind, including drunkenness, disorder, gambling, profanity and obscenity. Provisions were also made to keep high school kids from entering the pool parlors. Other former saloonkeepers waited because the sale of soft drinks and near beer would not come close to the profits made in the saloon trade.

Although the Upper Peninsula did not have distilleries, its numerous breweries were forced to close or change their direction. Charles Meeske had poured money into his Upper Peninsula Brewing Company in Marquette and created an efficient operation housed in a castle-like structure similar to those found along the Rhine River. Heartbroken, he refused to turn his property into a soft drink factory. Instead, he permanently closed the brewery and retired to California. However, others looked for new opportunities. The Calumet Brewing Company reopened producing soft drinks but was out of business within a year. The Escanaba Brewing Company stayed in business producing Neerit, a cereal beverage that was "a wholesome drink for the whole family." In its ad, it continued, "Easy to say—easier to drink—Neerit. Like needles are a household necessity. Drink Neerit with your meals or between meals." But this was not enough, and it closed after a short operation. The crosstown Richter Brewery created a new nonalcoholic

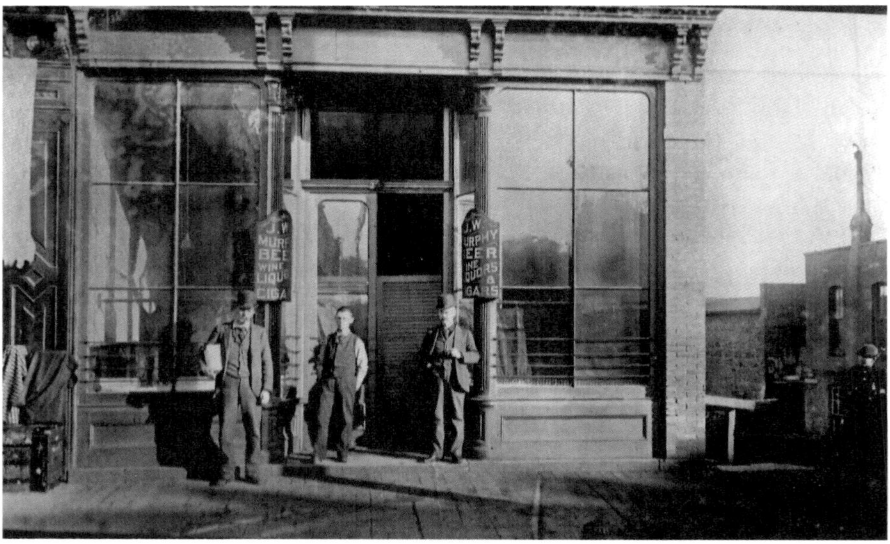

Murphy's Bar (1890) in Marquette has curtains and the lattice door to keep prying eyes from customers. During Prohibition, soft drink parlors' windows had to be kept unobstructed. *Courtesy of Marquette Regional History Center.*

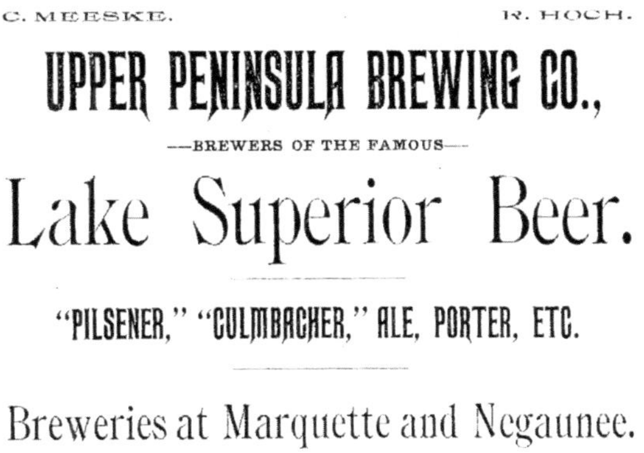

Left: An advertisement for the Upper Peninsula Brewing Company. *Courtesy of 906 Heritage, James Shefchik.*

Below: In Marquette, Charles Meeske was proud of his UP brewery, built like a castle, and refused to turn it into a soft drink factory. *Courtesy of Superior View.*

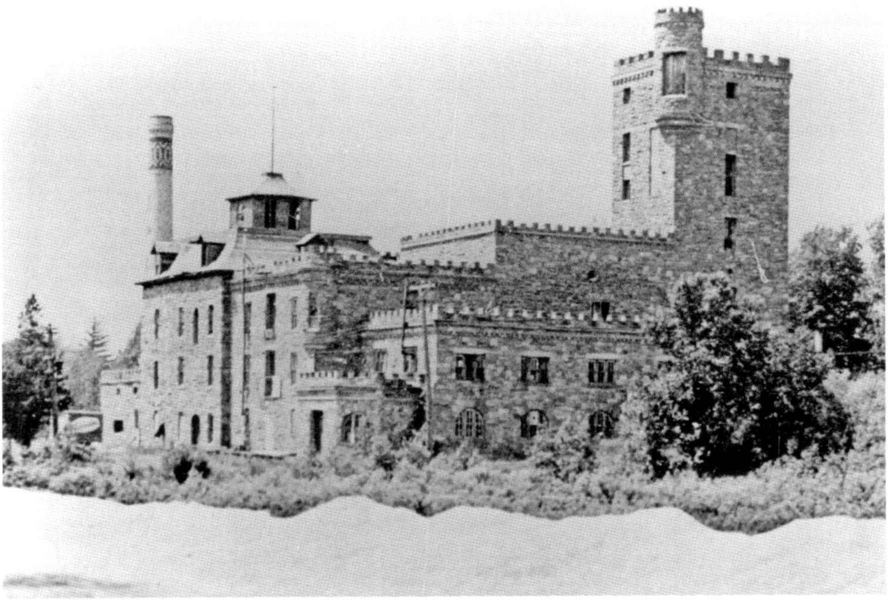

beverage, Ricto, which was made with pure water and the choicest cereals and had a hops flavor that gave it an aromatic taste. They stressed that it was locally made, and the community should support the local business. It also produced Whistle brand in a variety of flavors and remained in business through Prohibition. In Menominee, the two breweries Menominee River Brewing Company and Leisen and Henes combined their operations and created the United Beverage Company, which produced a nonalcoholic

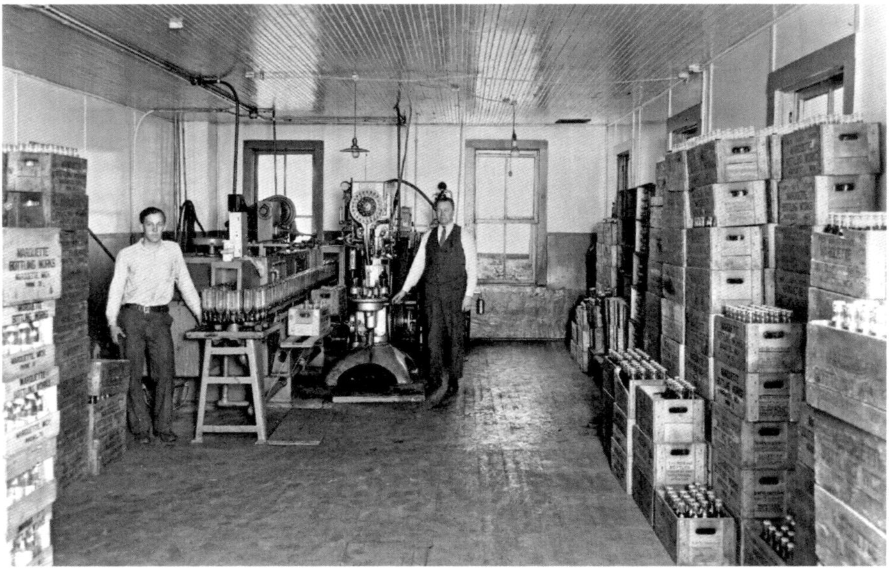

Marquette Bottling Works produced soft drinks demanded at speakeasies to mask the taste of moonshine. *Courtesy of Superior View.*

beverage called "Near Beer," later called "Silver Cream," and a variety of soft drinks. In Iron Mountain the Henze-Tollen Brewing Company consolidated with the Arbutus Beverage Company and created a line of soft drink beverages. The same was true of the Soo Brewing Company.

Avenues de Booze

Not to be denied, the bootlegger arose. Within hours of the advent of state prohibition, violations began. Although Michigan was now dry, neighboring Wisconsin remained wet until January 17, 1920. The three entry points—the "avenues de booze"—were, from east to west, Marinette, Wisconsin, opposite Menominee, Michigan; Florence, Wisconsin, opposite Iron Mountain, Michigan; and Hurley, Wisconsin opposite Ironwood, Michigan. Bootleggers and private citizens made the trip across the border for liquor. There was money to be made providing an illegal commodity.

The state police tried to close off these access routes, but even with the addition of sixteen men to the force, it was difficult. Violators were not only arrested near the border but also pulled over far from the border in the Marquette and copper country areas, often with whiskey in their cars.

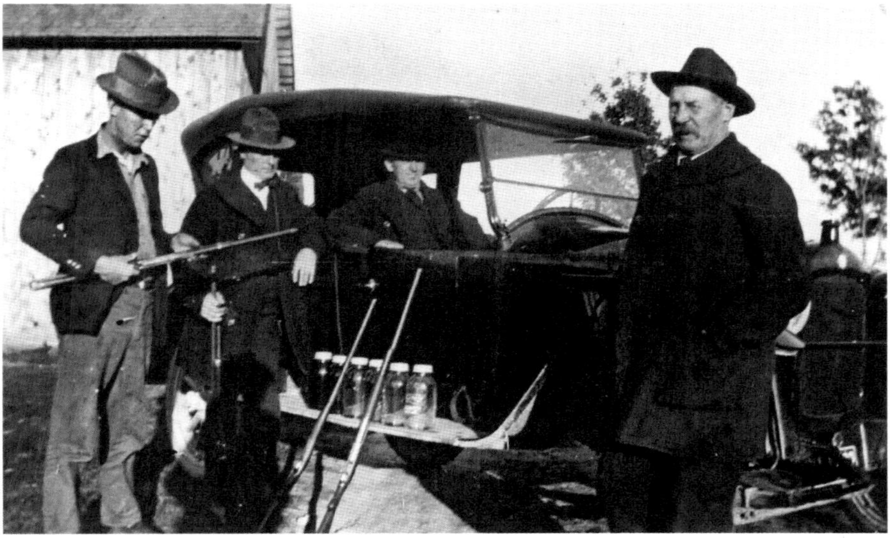

Federal Prohibition enforcement agents after a raid. *Courtesy of Superior View.*

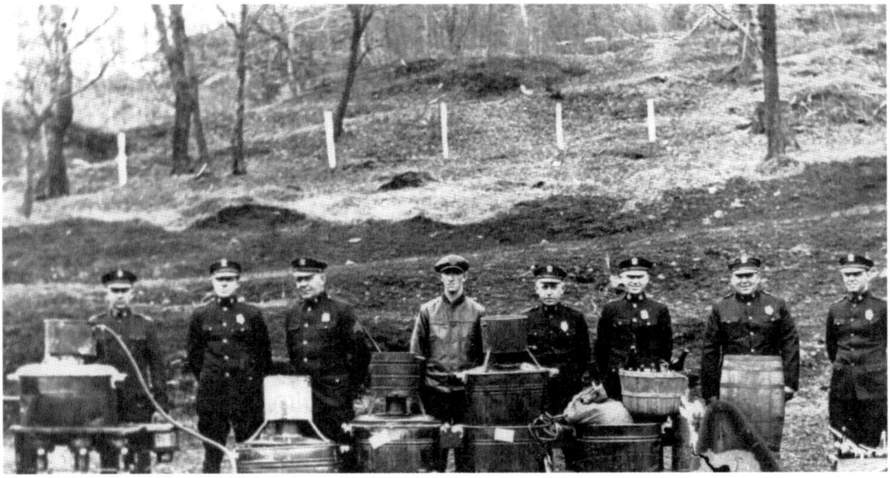

State and local police had their hands full with raids against moonshiners. *Courtesy of Superior View.*

HURLEY, WISCONSIN

Located on another border—the one with northern Wisconsin—is the community of Hurley, directly across the Montreal River from Ironwood, Michigan. These twin communities interacted with each other. Hurley came into being in 1885 as a railroad town where iron ore was loaded for transport to the docks in Ashland, some thirty miles to the west. Hurley became known as the vice city of the North because, given its isolation from the centers of power and population in Wisconsin, it went its merry way violating the law, even before the rise of Prohibition. A rough-and-tumble lumber town, it attracted lumberjacks and others seeking its wine, women and song. It became known as the "hell-hole of the range," and no boomtown from Duluth to Detroit could compete with its reputation for "sin, suffering, and saloons." It became a place that never observed Prohibition, and its infamous Silver Street operated day and night.

During Prohibition, there were nearly two hundred saloons disguised as soda shops lining its downtown streets. Northern Wisconsin became famous as a resort area beginning in the 1890s and, during Prohibition, attracted Chicago gangsters, who sought a quiet place to relax and fish, as well as operate gambling rackets, away from eye of the public and the FBI. Hurley became a favorite place for especially their lieutenants to recreate. Al Capone was unsuccessful in trying to make inroads into Hurley's well-established illegal booze business. It is said that he was a regular visitor to the area, and his brother Ralph operated several businesses in nearby Mercer and died in a Hurley nursing home.

For the Michigan State Police in 1921, Hurley was considered the "wettest" city in America; even federal enforcement agents could not bring it under control. Roy Vandercook, commander of the state police, said Hurley was "the booze headquarters for the upper country and was responsible for the greatest show of lawlessness in upper Michigan." Vandercook continued, "Hurley is the rottenest town I have ever heard of and I have my doubts about any prohibition enforcement." He concluded that if Hurley were cleaned up, Ironwood's criminal problems would be solved.

Obviously the immediate problem with enforcing state prohibition for Michigan law enforcement was Hurley. From 1918 through the start of national Prohibition in 1920 and beyond, Hurley provided liquor for some hundred miles along the Michigan-Wisconsin border. As a result, liquor was so common that people refused to be convinced that taking a drink was a capital offense!

During this period, liquor flowed across the porous border. In late September 1919, cases of Old Judge and Harper's whiskeys were easily shipped from Saxon, west of Hurley, to Bergland along the Duluth, South Shore & Atlantic (DSS&A) railroad. This became an important rumrunning route in the following years.

A number of Italian families from Hurley made their fortunes during Prohibition and then returned to Italy. The Fontecchio family left Hurley and migrated to an estate in the Abruzzi region, but they eventually returned to

Hurley. The Galbadini and Vezzetti families, from northern Italy, returned to their roots and remained, marrying into Italian nobility.

One nasty incident developed on the bridge across the Montreal River between Hurley and Ironwood in 1920. The state constabulary was stopping every car crossing the border. It could be said that these officers, recent veterans from World War I, were a bit overzealous in their enforcement. They attracted a crowd of Ironwoodians, who heckled them with the abusive epithet "slacker." Even when the local constable arrived to enforce city ordinances, the state police bypassed him, cracking heads and threatening the constable with "we'll get you." This incident was reported through the Upper Peninsula and was condemned by the editors of the *Marquette Mining Journal*, the *Ironwood Daily Globe* and other UP newspapers as an overreaction by the state police, who, they wrote, should be better trained to deal with the public. Colonel Vandercook, commander of the state police, went north to investigate and totally exonerated the police and said the constable was actually intoxicated and did not search any of the cars crossing into Michigan.

LIQUOR CACHES

At the onset of state prohibition, individuals stored up liquor supplies to hopefully outlast the ban. In July 1918, Emil Simonen of South Range, a former bartender who had "laid in a good supply," saw the police raid his home. They hauled out a typical supply: sixty-three gallons of whiskey, ninety-three gallons of beer, ten gallons of brandy and a case of bitters.

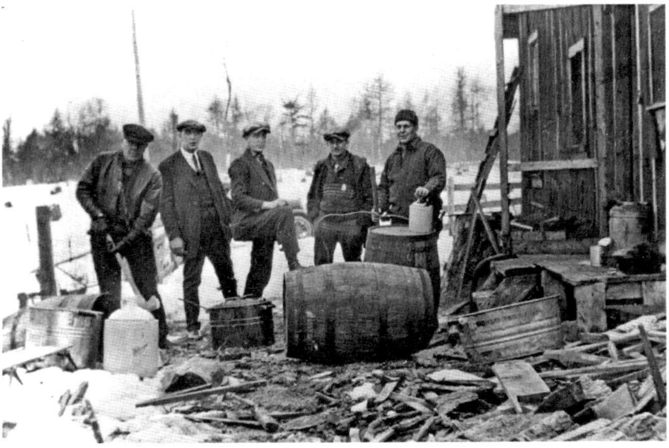

Prior to the coming of Prohibition, many people stocked up on liquor only to have enforcement raids seize it. *Courtesy of Superior View.*

Some wealthy individuals, hoping to make it through many holidays, created basements filled with pre-Prohibition liquor. However, many of these liquor hoards were raided by thieves over the years, leaving the owners helpless because they could not report the theft of illegal whiskey.

GRANOT LOMA AND THE KAUFMANS

A little-known private home from Prohibition days was built on the shore of Lake Superior north of Marquette: Granot Loma. It was the magnificent summer home of Louis and Marie Kaufman. Louis was an extremely successful Marquette and New York banker, who, among his many accomplishments, put together the financial packages that created General Motors and financed the Empire State Building. In 1919, he began the construction of what is considered the largest log cabin in the world based on the Adirondack camp tradition. State prohibition began in May 1918,

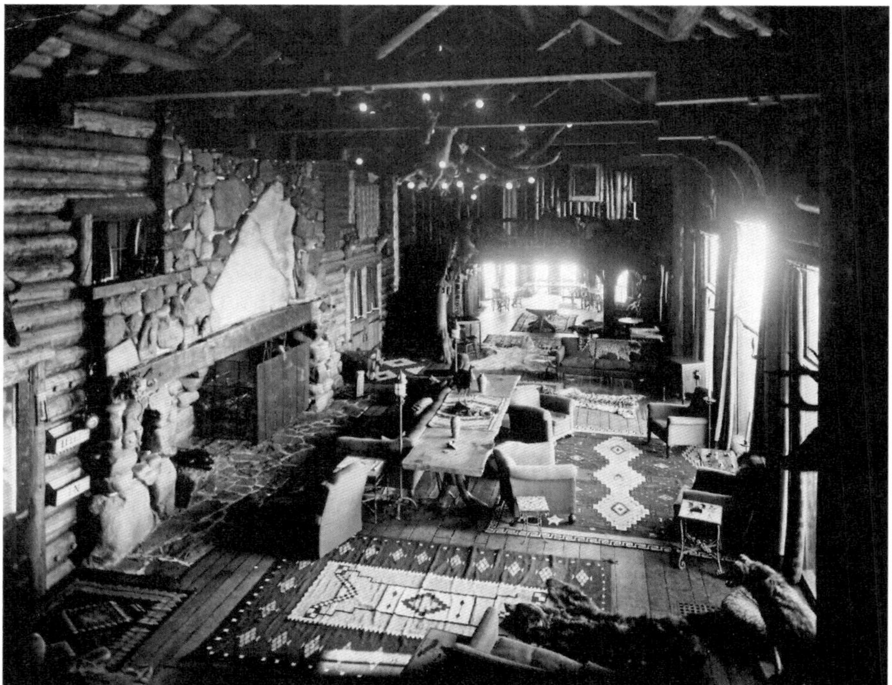

At Granot Loma, Hollywood and New York celebrities enjoyed the liquid hospitality of the Kaufmans. *Courtesy of Marquette Regional History Center.*

so Kaufman knew he had to quickly take action. He constructed two huge side-by-side bank vaults whose massive steel doors were marked "His" and "Hers." He and his wife, Marie, bought an entire liquor store in New York City and had the contents shipped by rail to the site. During the 1920s and 1930s, this stash of booze was used for parties they hosted for the rich and famous, who arrived by Kaufman's private rail car. Houseguests came from Hollywood to New York and included Fred Astaire, Mary Pickford, Lionel Barrymore, George Gershwin, Cole Porter, Pierre Du Pont, Max Schmeling and Sydney Sheldon. Metropolitan Opera tenors and sopranos entertained the guests from the balcony. Far from prying eyes, his guests could enjoy his magnificent estate and hospitality.

RUM REBELLION

In little over a month after the start of Prohibition, what should have been a minor incident turned into what was eventually called the "rum rebellion" and gained national headlines.

The center of the "rebellion" was Iron County, chiefly known as a center of lumbering and mining with many Italian and other immigrants. The Scalcucci brothers owned a three-story building in Iron River and made wine that was legal through a loophole in the Volstead Act. However, due to an abundance of grapes, they made more than the two-hundred-gallon limit. On February 14, 1920, the state police learned of the extra barrels of wine and raided the Scalcucci grocery store, seizing eight and a half barrels of wine. The prosecuting attorney Martin McDonough demanded that the wine be returned, as the officers did not have a warrant. This minor incident next involved the Prohibition Enforcement Agency, whose Chicago-based chief, Major A.V. Dalrymple, proclaimed, "Iron County is in open rebellion against prohibition." He headed north to end the rebellion with armed agents and arrest the Scalcuccis, McDonough and Iron County officials. The national commissioner defused the situation, but for over ten days, McDonough and Iron County were on the front pages of national newspapers. This is a fine example of the problem throughout the era with trying to implement the Volstead Act and avoid explosive rhetoric and actions.

MOONSHINING

The Upper Peninsula economy during Prohibition was wanting, and most people were unable to purchase and store vast quantities of liquor like Kaufman. They needed a relatively inexpensive supply. At first, newspapers carried ads captioned, "You Shouldn't Worry. Make Your Own," with the offer to supply a book of recipes for beer, whiskey, wines, et cetera, but this was soon declared in violation of the law. However, the reporter concluded in December 1919 that "almost everyone has a recipe in his pocket, introduced since Michigan went dry and the ingredients are in almost every case commodities used for cooking purposes." Shops selling hops, barley syrups and extracts, yeast, corn meal and other supplies and apparatus opened. Although it was illegal to openly promote home-brewing, all of the major breweries, including Pabst, Anheuser-Busch and Brumalt, advertised for sale barley extract and syrup in three-pound cans for baking and cooking. However, when they advertised both "plain and hop flavored," it was obvious that they were selling their product for home-brewing—but still legal!

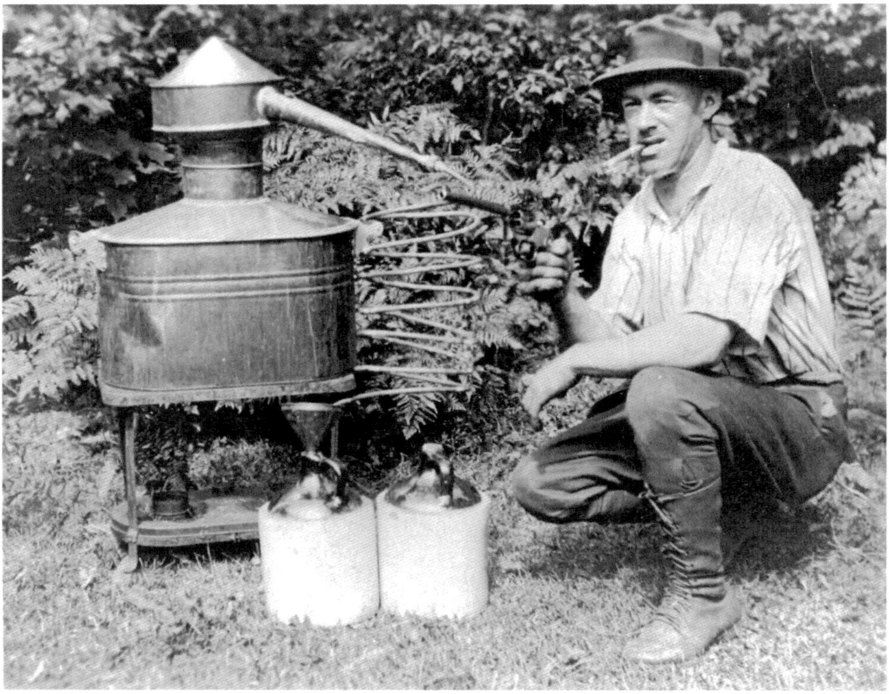

Revolver-armed Herman Nelson was typical of moonshiners who operated throughout the Upper Peninsula. *Courtesy of Marquette Regional History Center.*

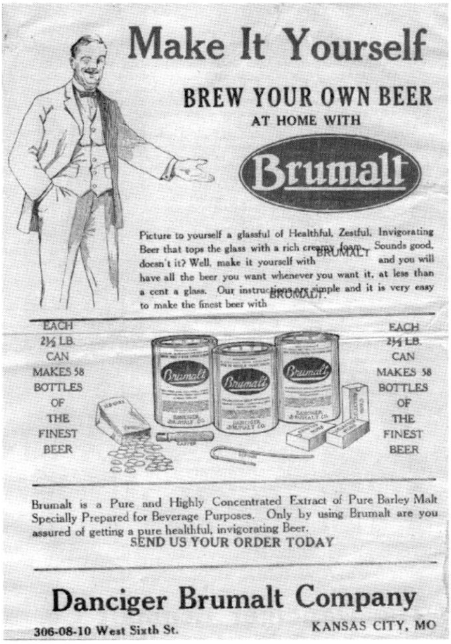

Brumalt was promoted as a barley syrup for cooking and baking, but home-brewers knew better. *Courtesy of Still Picture Unit National Archives.*

Winemaking was legal but limited to two hundred gallons per household annually and only to be consumed by the family. Train cars filled with grapes continued to reach the UP. To help the California vintners, the federal government provided funding so that grape bricks of concentrated grape juice could be made. Companies like Vino Santo out of San Francisco shipped these bricks east with a warning on the side of the box: "After dissolving the brick in a gallon of water, do not place the liquid in a jug away in the cupboard for 20 days, because then it would turn to wine." Later they even listed the flavor—burgundy, claret, port and sherry. Another company, Vino-Glo, merely alerted the buyer, "For home use only." This is another example of the hypocrisy connected with Prohibition. Soon thousands of homes across the nation and the UP became small distilleries, breweries and wineries.

There were a number of reasons for development of local stills. The price of imported liquor brought in by bootleggers or rumrunners from Canada was expensive, as was any liquor that had to be protected with bribes and transportation costs. This overhead raised the price of highballs in Chicago from a pre-Prohibition price of fifteen cents a glass to seventy-five cents during Prohibition.

The production of moonshine is usually associated with the Scotch-Irish tradition of Appalachia, but it can flourish anywhere. The production of beer or liquor is merely the process of fermentation. You need water, corn meal, cane sugar and yeast, which you mix and let ferment before running it through a still. The result is a high-proof unaged liquor sometimes called "white lightning" or "white mule."

Any early tradition of moonshining in the Upper Peninsula is unrecorded, but probably the earliest distillers were French Canadians. Late nineteenth-century Italian immigrants made wine and then took the waste grapes, or

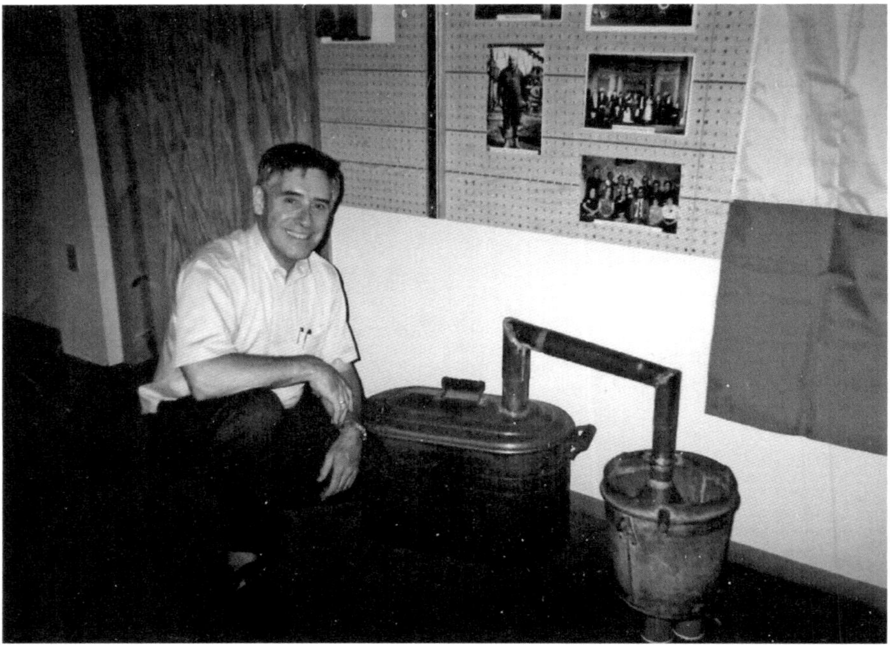

The laundry washer was used to distill grappa at Duke of Abruzzi Club, Caspian, Michigan. *Courtesy of R.M. Magnaghi.*

pomace, added sugar, let it ferment and distilled a very potent white liquor called grappa. Traditionally, they drank it after dinner as a *digestif* or, on a cold day, at breakfast with coffee, which was known as coffee royal.

The arrival of woodchoppers from Kentucky prior to 1918 brought their moonshining expertise, which they shared with locals. Moonshining was extensively carried on throughout the Upper Peninsula, a region with plenty of room to hide the stills deep in the woods or swamps. Moonshiners were aided by roads that, in some remote locations, were mere trails and, in others, nearly impassable.

Although moonshine was produced throughout the UP, Delta County and the city of Escanaba were considered the wettest areas in the UP by state officials. This development fit into the traditional attitude of the community, seen in an election in April 1916, when residents voted 1,828 wet and 883 dry. Most people opposed prohibition, which would cut city revenue and raise property taxes.

Despite the size of the territory, county sheriffs, state police and Federal Prohibition Enforcement agents scoured the countryside and were, in many cases, successful in their efforts. In mid-August 1923, the Delta

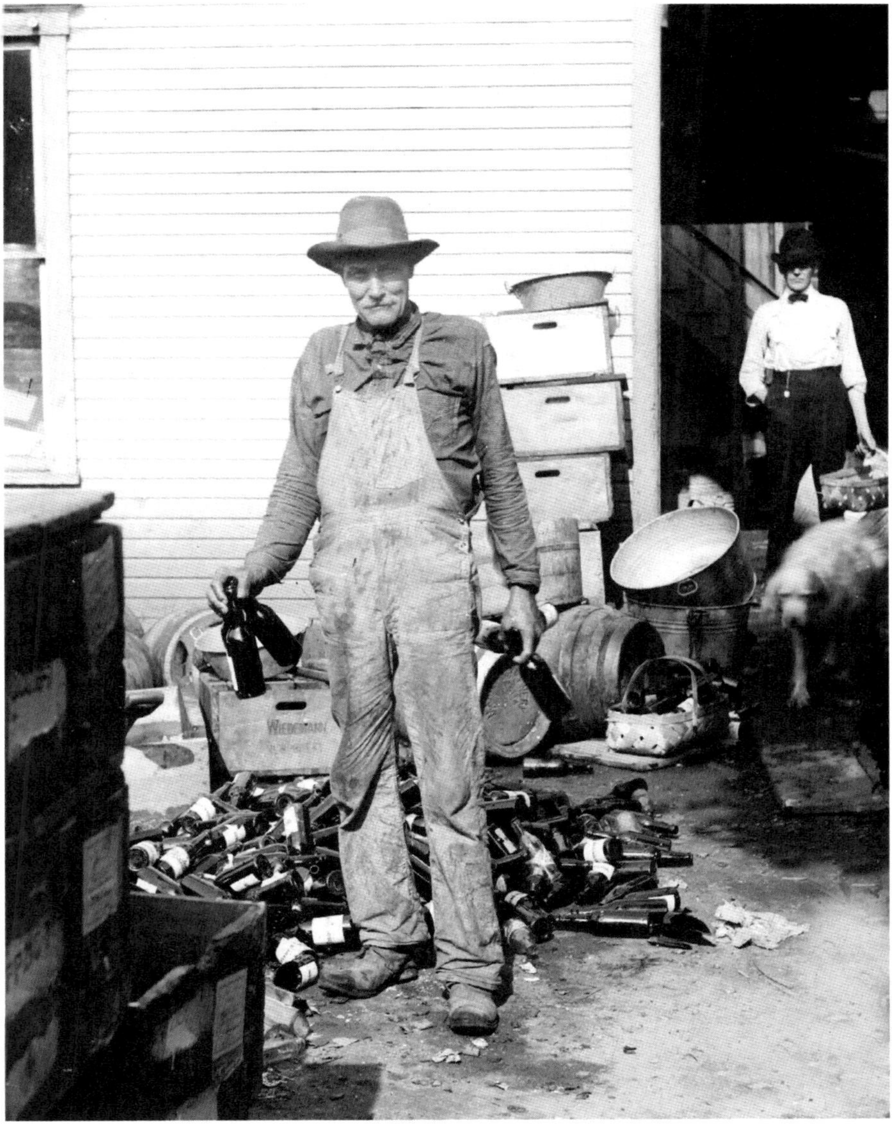

Some moonshine was kept for evidence in a forthcoming trial, but the bulk was destroyed. *Courtesy of Superior View.*

County sheriff and federal agents raided a still set in the dense woods ten miles northeast of Rapid River. They uncovered two monster stills with 200-gallon capacities that produced 75 gallons of moonshine daily. The entire outfit comprised the largest illicit plant ever turned up in the UP and included 1,500 gallons of fermenting corn and 90 gallons of the finished

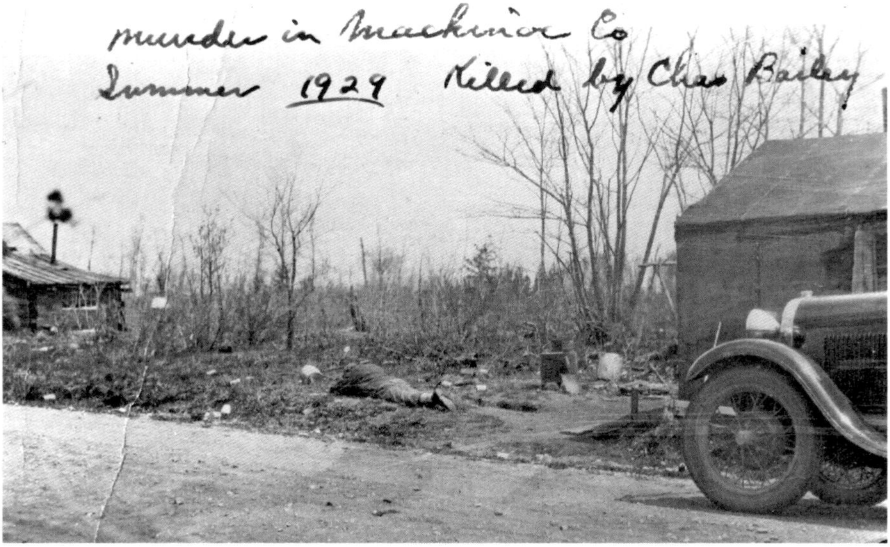

Violence and death were ever-present hazards to the illegality connected with Prohibition. *Courtesy of Superior View.*

product. The distillers fled at the sound of the autos and did not return, although the police waited all night for them. The equipment and mash were destroyed and the barrels burned.

Stills not only were operated in the woods but also found their way into basements in town. One fellow in Escanaba improvised a large cellar in two adjoining homes and set his still to work. Unfortunately, the police smelled the telltale fumes coming through the cracks and raided the operation. Others had secret rooms constructed in homes and barns to hide their operations. One such barn in Brimley in the eastern UP was so well hidden that it was discovered only in the spring of 2015. There always was the fear that the smell of distilling or brewing would attract the police. A fellow in Schoolcraft County had a cabin on an island where he made his moonshine; the island location was ideal because it had the added protection of the water. In 1923, the sanitation department of Escanaba and later Ishpeming reported that the main sewers were plugged with mash and would have to be cleaned weekly. Other communities had similar costly problems in their sewers.

Most of the moonshine produced was considered poor quality. However, there are stories that gang members from Chicago and Detroit looked to the UP to locate their stills up north. Memories persist of Raymbaultown and Swedetown, suburbs of Calumet where Italian and Slovenian immigrants produced high-quality liquor. It is said that the

Chicago market paid dearly for this moonshine when a dealer learned "it's from Raymbaultown." One story often repeated had a group of boys playing at a corner in Raymbaultown when a large black car approached them and stopped. A fellow stepped out dressed in a dark suit and hat and approached the youngsters, who knew what was going on and were frightened by the appearance of what they rightly considered a gangster. When he asked, "Who makes booze around here," the kids were hesitant. Then one boy stepped forward and said, "Do you see that house on the corner? It is the only one that doesn't produce shine."

In Raymbaultown, moonshine was made in basements with windows covered with thick curtains. While production was underway, wives sat and socialized on the porch. With the approach of a new officer, one who had not been "gifted" with a bottle of dago red or grappa, the alert was given, and the basement went silent.

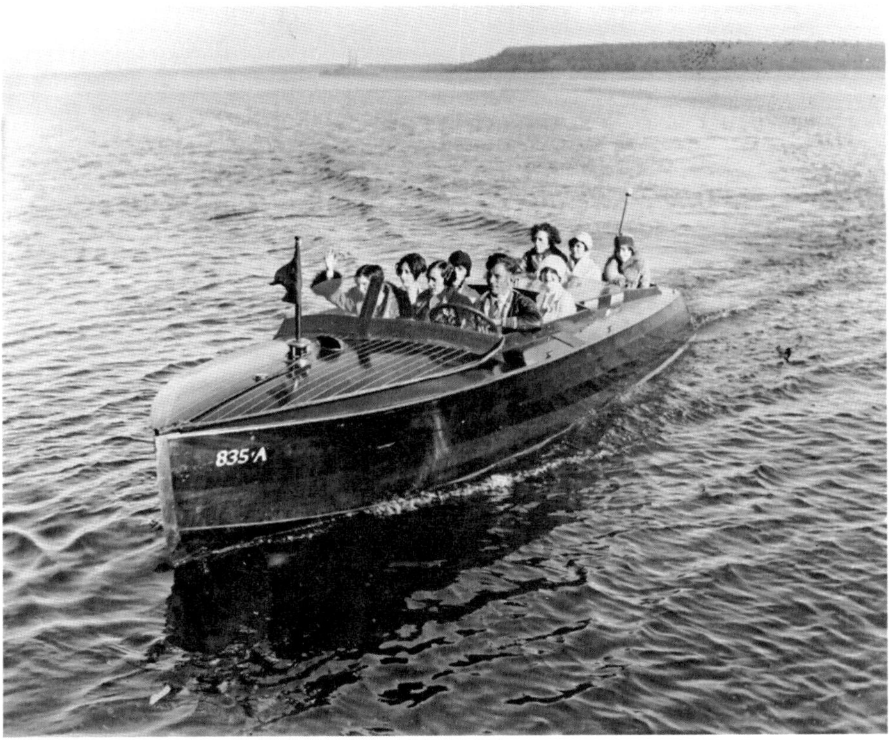

Speedboats built by Chris Craft and Hacker Craft took visitors around Mackinac Island during the day and ran booze from Canada at night. *Courtesy of Mackinac Island State Park.*

Since both Mackinac and Bois Blanc were islands and somewhat isolated, they became focal points for moonshining. Bois Blanc Island was sparsely populated, but there were at least three local moonshiners operating on the island, as well as some Kentuckian shiners. A.L. Todd, a Harvard graduate, had land on the west end of the island and was aided by Kentuckians. He delivered his moonshine to Mackinac under the cover of a load of firewood. It was stored in the back storage room of Donnelly's market for resale. John Bible also had a still on Bois Blanc, as did "Pea Soup" Cadreau. These moonshiners were careful to buy their corn at the Arnold dock and sugar in J.W. Davis & Sons store to avoid suspicion of what they were doing.

Moonshining became the major industry on the island, especially at Harrisonville, where a still was operated by the justice of the peace. Again to avoid police detection, the Mackinac bootleggers bought their sugar and grain at St. Ignace.

Prohibition had a notable effect on the economy of Mackinac Island. Shops that sold beer, not wanting to operate illegally, turned to soft drinks. The only blind pig on the island was the Cannonball, located at English Landing, a significant distance from the main part of town. Bill Chambers operated a "nice place" and did a thriving business. A pool hall at the current location of Horn's Bar and Grill sold moonshine on the second floor while a soda shop was on the street level. There was a general feeling among the local population that Prohibition had a negative effect on the island, and things went downhill. The bars and taverns were closed, and the "sporting" people stopped coming during the summer. Many of the affluent headed for Canadian waters in the North Channel, where they could imbibe without a surprise visit from federal agents.

BAD MOONSHINE

Most moonshine was not of the best quality. It was produced without government supervision and usually not overseen by a trained chemist. To get an added "kick," moonshiners would add manure, bleach, rubbing alcohol, paint thinner or urine, among other things. In their hasty production, they would not distill it two to three times to remove impurities. Due to faulty equipment and unsanitary conditions, they created toxic alcohol. The chance of getting the "real stuff" was no better than eight in one hundred, and poorly made moonshine led to blindness and/or death.

In early March 1920, a group of men went to the Hillberg camp four miles from Watson. Joseph Shepherd, an itinerant bootlegger, showed up and sold his homemade moonshine to the men. After drinking the poison, the men fell violently ill and then died one by one over the weekend. Both the sheriff and state police were soon on Shepherd's trail for the murders he committed.

The state police and the Michigan Food and Drug Commission oversaw the implementation of Prohibition enforcement. As a result, samples of moonshine were frequently sent to commission labs. Their findings were frightening; much of what was sent proved to be poisonous and deadly. One chemist at Michigan Tech, after testing a sample of moonshine, asked if the drinker had survived. Fred L. Woodworth, commissioner in the early days, sent out warnings to alert the public to the deadly nature of moonshine, but many people felt that these were warnings to frighten people into obeying the Volstead Act and kept drinking.

BOOTLEGGER

The making of home-brew and moonshine and the importation of foreign liquor were underway, but that left the task of delivery. The solution to the transportation problem gave rise to the "Whiskey Six," which referred to a six-cylinder Studebaker, Buick and other cars that were sturdy and fast, able to travel over rough roads at ninety miles an hour "like a thunderbolt." By removing the rear seat, reinforcing the chassis and adding leveling springs, they could carry as many as one hundred cases of liquor, remain level and not attract police attention. On some, headlights turned with the steering wheel, which aided travel through twisty UP roads and trails. Other autos carried liquor in spare tires, special double gas tanks, specially built fenders and hidden compartments. As one reporter noted, it was best to have a cheaper car like a Model-T because the police were less likely to take notice.

Those on foot also became creative to avoid detection. One fellow hauled ten gallons of liquor in a trunk by rail while another struggled with a new suitcase filled with booze. Both were caught. Liquor passed across the UP on the Duluth, South Shore & Atlantic Railroad that was under control of the Canadian Pacific Railway. Trains crossed the St. Mary's River from the Canadian to the American Soo. Porters and dining car attendants were known to bring in small quantities of liquor. For the thrill of evading the

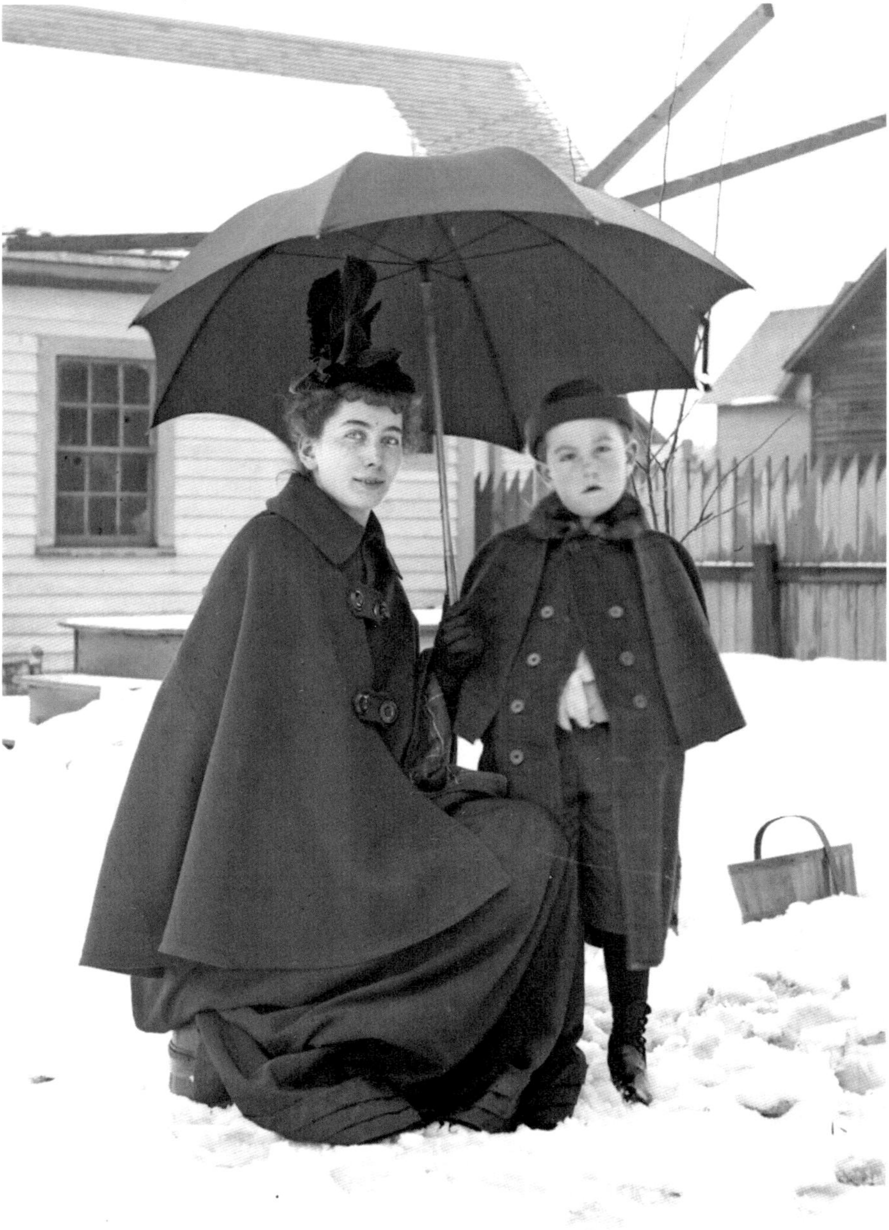

Long coats and umbrellas provided cover for delivering moonshine in town. *Courtesy of Superior View.*

law, some women put flasks in their garters and stockings and crossed on the ferry or carried hot water bottles filled with booze. Men and women wore specially altered coats that were lined with small liquor bottle pockets. Many people carried a hip flask in case they needed a quick shot. Liquor moved about in burlap sacks, cardboard cartons, lifeboats, coal piles, suitcases and trunks, hidden in caches of freight cargo and anywhere agents and police would not expect it. Liquor was hidden under coal and wood piles on ships.

Possession of even the smallest amount of alcohol would cause an arrest, and as a result, bribes or what amounted to "gifts" ruled the day. Local and state police, federal enforcement agents and Coast Guardsmen were poorly paid and sought a quick fix to "look the other way."

There was also the passage of large quantities of liquor shipped as evidence to federal court usually from Marquette to Sault Ste. Marie. In mid-July 1920, Leo Grove's vault of confiscated liquor—medicinal, bonded, ordinary whiskey, moonshine, "tanglefoot" and "sure death" along with a variety of bitters, patent medicines, cordials and liqueurs—had to be sent to Sault Ste. Marie, Michigan, as evidence in federal court. The shipment filled an express car on the DSS&A, and when it was shipped at an undisclosed time, it was heavily guarded by federal agents fearing a holdup or train wreck. As a *Mining Journal* reporter quipped, "It is estimated that the alcohol content of the assortment has heat sufficient to weld the two propeller-blades broken on the recent trip of the *Noronic*."

Capone and the Northern Border

The accounts and myths of Al Capone's presence and sightings in the Upper Peninsula are innumerable. Why would these stories continue to be told? There is a strong likelihood that Capone visited this border region with Canada because of his strong rumrunning and bootlegging connections. Lake Superior was considered "Al Capone's northern gateway," and he was a large customer of Canadian Club whiskey.

It is reputed that Capone had a vacation home at Couderay, Wisconsin, and that seaplanes flew in booze from Canada. Rumors persist that he was a guest at the Four Seasons Resort on Miscuano Island on the Menominee River near Pembine, Wisconsin.

The epicenter of Capone connections is Escanaba. He was alleged to have had a home there, and a reputable story is told of him buying a pack of cigarettes at a shop in North Escanaba owned by John Stasewich and leaving money so Stasewich could give local kids candy. One unsubstantiated story from Sault Ste. Marie tells of a grandmother serving a meal to Capone. There are other stories of Chicago gangsters being sent north to hideout on an island in Little Lake until the heat back home "quieted down." There is also a more substantiated story that Capone kept a black boat, the *Norco*, which carried liquor from Batchawana Bay to Whitefish Point for shipment to Chicago.

REPLACEMENTS FOR LIQUOR

Although relatively inexpensive moonshine was locally produced and available, people looked to alcoholic products on their store shelves. On the eve of state prohibition, there were discussions in UP newspapers concerning the sale of patent medicines, toilet and antiseptic preparations or solutions and flavoring for beverages. Michigan officials were looking to state Supreme Court decisions concerning these preparations to serve as a guide for prosecutors.

As early as December 1919, drugstores in the copper country and elsewhere cut off the sale of Hoffman drops since they were not being purchased for medicinal purposes. The same held true for various patent medicines that contained a high percentage of alcohol.

One of the alternatives was Jamaica ginger, a patent medicine with 93 to 96 percent alcohol that, at the start of Prohibition, was consumed with water as a cocktail called gingerie. However, by early 1921, the federal government had stepped in, and the original version of Jamaican ginger was available only by prescription. A nasty-tasting version ordered by the government was available without prescription. One reporter said that it went down like "molten lead." Hoffman drops consisted of two parts alcohol and one part ether. Lemon extract (85 percent alcohol) was frequently mixed with coffee. There were other extracts, such as peppermint, cinnamon, almond and mint, that were available but frequently bypassed. Wine of pepsin (29 percent alcohol), a stomach medicine, was favored by others. Angostura bitters were a safe and a somewhat palatable stomachache remedy with a 90 percent alcohol content. It was served throughout the UP.

These extracts were based on the idea that "a reasonable person" would not use them as an alcoholic beverage. One firefighter in Negaunee literally hid hundreds of boxes in his basement filled with small empty bottles of Jamaica ginger. The average person did not know the chemical reactions of these extracts. A fellow from Au Train drank canned heat (sterno), which is poisonous due to the addition of denatured alcohol, but survived and told the police in Marquette it had a "good kick" to it. Others were not deterred and drank wood alcohol (poisonous methanol) and prune juice and survived, though blindness could be a result. Not everyone was this lucky. On a June day in 1920, Jacob Penttinen of Cleveland Location in Ishpeming went out with friends on a road project, and when they were done they decided to have a party. Later in the day, Jacob stumbled into a soft drink shop, sat for a few minutes and then fell over dead. He had consumed a deadly cocktail composed of moonshine, Hoffman drops and corn remover.

PRESCRIPTION ALCOHOL

As we have seen, some of these patent medicines were available through prescription. Druggists could dispense alcohol with a physician's prescription that had to be kept on file for two years, and they had to submit monthly reports. Failure to follow the law could result in loss of license, $1,000 fine and a year in jail. This was an expensive proposition—the prescription cost three dollars and a pint three dollars while you could buy a gallon of moonshine for four dollars. The prescription racket was so flagrant that some physicians signed blank prescriptions and left them with the pharmacist, who filled in the order as needed.

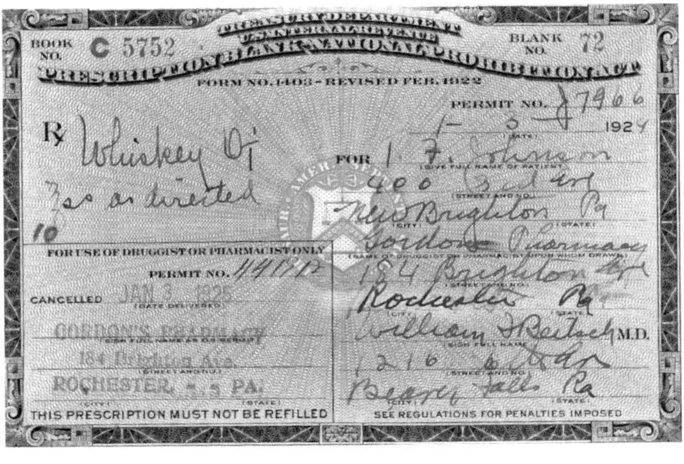

Physicians prescribed whiskey for medicinal reasons. *Courtesy of Still Picture Unit National Archives.*

ENFORCEMENT

The Anti-Saloon League and others promoting Prohibition took the position that as it was a constitutional amendment, the public would readily obey the law and saloons and liquor would be a thing of the past. This radical social and cultural change did not take hold and was disregarded. It was obvious that Congress felt this way because originally only $12 million was appropriated for enforcement throughout the United States.

The major unit enforcing the Volstead Act was the Federal Prohibition Enforcement Agency, which was supposed to work in tandem with state police and then county and city police. The federal agency's headquarters for the Upper Peninsula was in the Federal Building in downtown Marquette, and its first chief agent was Leo J. Grove from Ovid, Michigan. Grove was a hardworking official who avoided sensationalism and the media. By 1924, he was still chief agent and one of the longest-serving chiefs in the United States. Grove headed a force of about a half dozen men who had to oversee 16,452 square miles of the UP. Two of his men patrolled the Canadian border aided by U.S. Customs and the Coast Guard, obviously a job beyond their capability. The Coast Guard, under the Treasury Department, was charged with enforcing smuggling laws, which included rumrunning. The level of enforcement depended on individual commanders, who had twenty- to thirty-year-olds in their command who undoubtedly enjoyed a drink or two.

There were other chief enforcement agents who operated out of Marquette. In 1927, T.T. Hurley was the chief agent and used informants, "secret service agents" and investigators to find illegal operations. He was followed by Ray W. Harring who lasted for thirteen months, until his failure to pass the Civil Service examination caused him to resign in the spring of 1930. The last chief agent was Oscar C. Rummler, who had formerly served in Grand Rapids. During his term in office he led a number of successful raids in the western UP. However, as Prohibition began to wind down in mid-1933, he lost his agents and was the main enforcement agent. His position terminated with the end of Prohibition in December 1933.

Wages were low. A Coast Guard recruit made $21 a week. The agents were also poorly paid, with some making $40 to $50 weekly or $1,200 annually. Bribes were not out of the question, and some saw the enforcement agency as a "training school for bootleggers."

The public both despised and feared the federal agents, but the general distaste for them was moderated by their limited numbers and ability to be

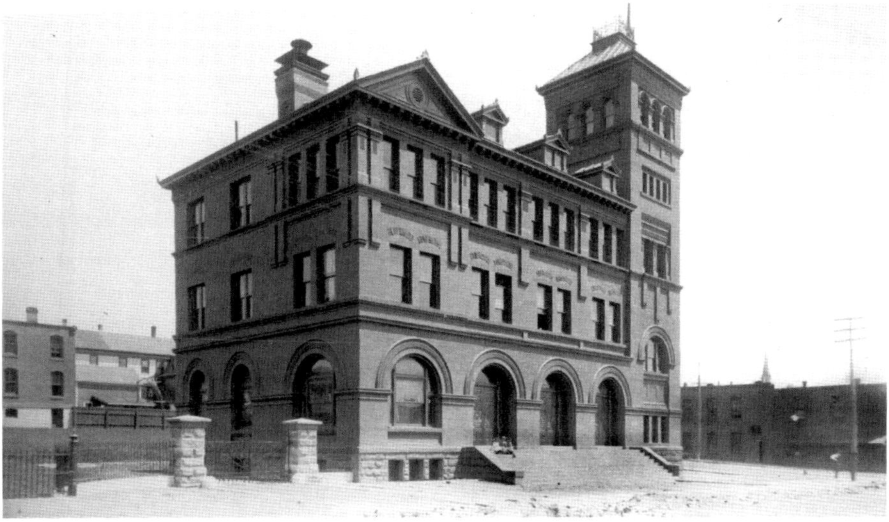

Leo Grove, head of the Federal Prohibition Enforcement Agency in the UP, was headquartered in the Federal Building in Marquette. *Courtesy of Superior View.*

bribed. At the same time, the agents had to cope with a flood of illegal beer and spirits. In some cases, the agents kept a low profile and made raids only when there were too many complaints.

Records give us a view of an active honest agent, John Saul (1868–1941). He began his term in office on January 1, 1920, and became a dedicated agent who worked with sheriffs. He avoided sensational exploits, arrested more violators than anyone in the district and had the largest percentage of convictions. He got real results in every sector where he worked and was praised by his boss Leo Grove and federal judge Clarence W. Sessions. When he resigned to take a city position at Manistique, he had been on the force the longest of any agent—one year, ten months and fifteen days—and thus was burned out from his job.

DARK SIDE: JOHN E. FILLION

Then there was the dark side of agents connected with Prohibition enforcement. The short career of John E. Fillion in 1920–21 is one of the most deplorable and shows the lengths that agents would go to cash in on Prohibition. Fillion was based out of Marquette and was a brash individual who bullied his way through life. While on duty in Escanaba in June 1920, he proceeded to stop men on the streets trying to implicate them in bootlegging. After a number of incidents, he was given a warrant to appear in court by police sergeant Joe Carney. Outraged by this action of a lowly policeman, Fillion drew his Colt 45, and Carney pulled out his pistol. Disarmed and on the way to court, he broke down and begged Carney to save his skin. In court, he was charged with carrying a concealed weapon, pointing a gun at T.J. Prouex, assault and battery of John Sharkey and pointing a loaded gun at a police officer. The trial was concluded at a later date, but the conviction was never covered in the papers. Some ten days later, he and agent H.C. Ashmun seized $18,000 (about $213,224 today) worth of liquor at Florence, Wisconsin, and were bringing it to Bessemer when they were stopped by a local sheriff unaware of who they were. An altercation was avoided, and they moved on only to have a flat tire, veered off the road and, as a result, broke most of the bottles.

Despite all of these incidents, Fillion was regarded in Marquette, where he lived with his family, as a hero who was cunning and shrewd in working with bootleggers and understood their business. However, stories and reports coming from Hurley, where he was supposed to be enforcing Prohibition, painted a different picture. It was said that he appeared on the street drunk and worked in bars, but Fillion explained that it was part of his disguise to catch violators. The family man never explained his involvement with local prostitutes, nor could he explain the hush money taken from local saloonkeepers.

In October, he was involved in an elaborate plot in which he double-crossed the Hurley bootleggers and the Prohibition agency. He told his boss, Grove, that he was rounding up bootleggers. On the other hand, he promised the Hurley saloonkeepers "protection, using the badge of a federal officer to attain this end"—namely, bringing several hundred cases of alcohol north from Milwaukee. He led eight Studebakers (Whiskey Sixes) south and, despite taking an oath to uphold the Constitution, bought the liquor at a warehouse outside Milwaukee and headed back to Hurley. On the return trip, he told Grove of the run, and south of Hurley on the night of October 9, federal agents tried to stop the liquor convoy. In the process, they shot and killed John M. Chiapuzio. The story gets complicated, with Fillion stealing liquor, selling it and returning to Marquette. This incident was the last straw. A federal warrant for malfeasance in office and transporting liquor was issued, and Fillion was fired on December 18. Leaving his bills unpaid,

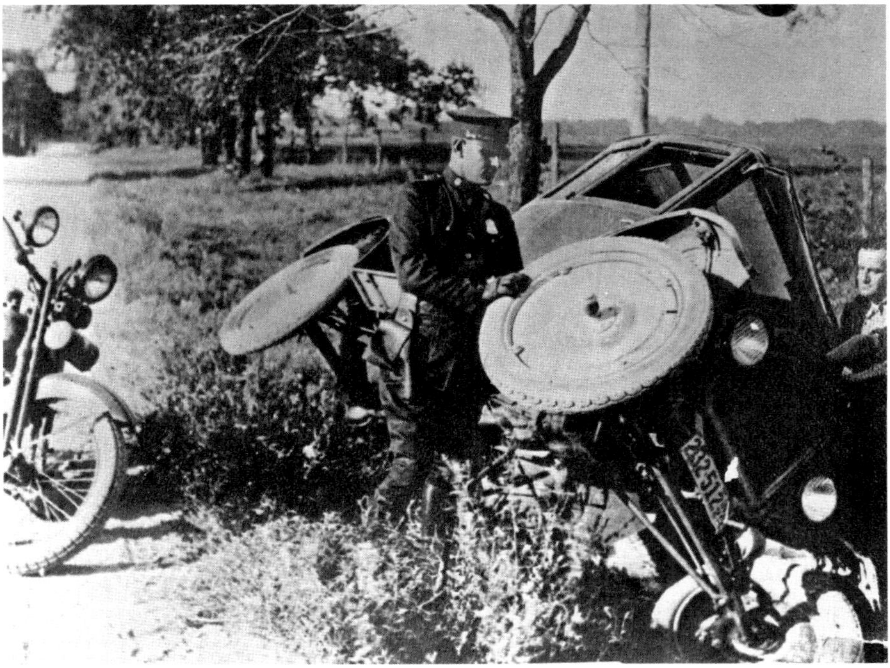

Due to the profits connected with bootlegging, hijacking and violence were common, and bribes were paid to the police to keep them at bay. *Courtesy of Superior View.*

he gathered his family, and they headed for Sault Ste. Marie and Canada, hopefully beyond federal law. He eventually returned to the United States but was never tried for his involvement in the murder of Chiapuzio.

FEDERAL COURT AND CONVICTIONS

At the start of Prohibition, the federal court for the Western District of Michigan was in charge of implementing the Volstead Act. Judge Clarence W. Sessions (1859–1931), who had been on the bench since 1911, brought the full weight of the law on violators and made a number of groundbreaking decisions from the bench in Marquette and Sault Ste. Marie.

In October 1920, ten months after the start of Prohibition, Judge Sessions set the tone for his court with the warning, "It is time that men should know that an act of Congress is to be obeyed and not violated." At that point, he sentenced twenty-three violators to detentions of thirty days to six months at the Detroit House of Corrections and gave fines ranging from $100 to $500 as additional penalty.

In his deliberations, Judge Sessions took into consideration all of the circumstances surrounding each case and considered whether a man had a family, the character of his offense and whether his liquor dealings were commercial or for private use.

Judge Sessions initiated the first case on record in the United States where defendants on trial for liquor law violations were convicted not merely for transporting whiskey but also for conspiracy against the federal government. By November 1922, Judge Sessions was imposing stiff prison sentences with the goal of bringing liquor law violations to an end. Editorials agreed that prison sentencing was the only way to stop widespread liquor traffic. In May 1922, federal judge Arthur Tuttle cleaned up cases at the Sault Ste. Marie. Forty- three men were given sentences, which sent them to the Detroit House of Corrections and to the federal prison at Leavenworth, Kansas. The editor of the *Mining Journal* concluded that this action had the potential "to win respect for statute." Howard A. Quirt, editor and publisher of the *Ironwood Daily Globe*, said that this action would make the UP dry and continued, "The moonshine industry continues highly remunerative, but the stern attitude of courts is making the game not worth the powder. Fines are one thing; prison sentences are another."

All of these prison sentences and hopeful ink did little to end liquor law violations. By mid-October 1924, the number of indictments in federal court at Marquette had risen to seventy-nine dealing with liquor law violations and one concerned with postal fraud.

If Judge Sessions was enforcing Prohibition through his convictions, this was not the case of all judges. Recorder's Court judge Chris Stein in Detroit said that he was wasting his time with liquor cases and rid his court of most of them. Judges did not have a specific policy to follow when handing out jail terms, and in the UP, they did not follow a hard-and-fast policy. Judge Richard C. Flannigan (1859–1928) in Marquette took the position that if liquor violations also involved prostitution, delivering liquor from a school bus, selling liquor at a gas station, which could lead to an accident, or chronic liquor violations, stronger sentences were meted out. Flanagan felt that first-time offenders who were let off with a fine might think twice about further violations of the law; plus, he had to deal with crowded jails. The Marquette jail became overcrowded, and prisoners had to be sent to Traverse City and Detroit. So depending on the judge, local judges tended to be more lenient than federal judges.

Then the Michigan legislature passed the habitual criminal law that went into effect on September 5, 1927, and provided judges with no discretion. This applied to liquor violators. On their fourth offense, they were given automatic life sentences. It was referred to as "life for a pint" and "life for liquor." Tony Popich of Manistique was the first person in the UP to be convicted. His earlier convictions went back to 1924, so when the police found moonshine and wine in his home, Judge Herbert W. Runnels had to sentence Popich to life at Jackson. Upon sentencing, Popich wept but soon recovered and joked with his guards, "If you'd buy my ticket, I'll go down to Jackson alone."

This law was controversial, especially as it affected liquor violators, although the Anti-Saloon League heartily supported it. Governor Fred Green opposed it, and soon the legislature modified the crimes to be included, permitting Popich's release.

STATE POLICE

On the state level, the front line of defense for enforcing the Michigan prohibition law was the Michigan Constabulary, later known as the state police, created on April 19, 1917. Headquartered in the UP at Negaunee and Bessemer, its initial mission in the Upper Peninsula was to see that radical laborers did not close the iron mines during World War I. However, this mission was expanded with the coming of state prohibition on May 1, 1918. By legislative action in 1921, the state police were to apprehend and arrest Prohibition violators, and the State Food and Drug Department was authorized to dispose of the alcohol.

Over the years of Prohibition, the state police remained active and improved their ability to implement the law. Some of them went undercover and got evidence. George Uthe in 1921 was so busy at the Sault Ste. Marie that he had little time to shave. This worked well for him, as he donned heavy lumberjack clothes and with his silver badge concealed on his suspenders proceeded to enter speakeasies and close them down. Also at the Sault Ste. Marie, trooper Frank Sidek presented himself at the home of Louis Belanger seeking whiskey for his hunting camp. In a subsequent police raid, a large quantity of alcohol was found in Belanger's house, and he was arrested. In a sweep of the Princeton–Little Lake area south of Marquette, the troopers confiscated a large quantity of moonshine, "molasses wine," raisin mash,

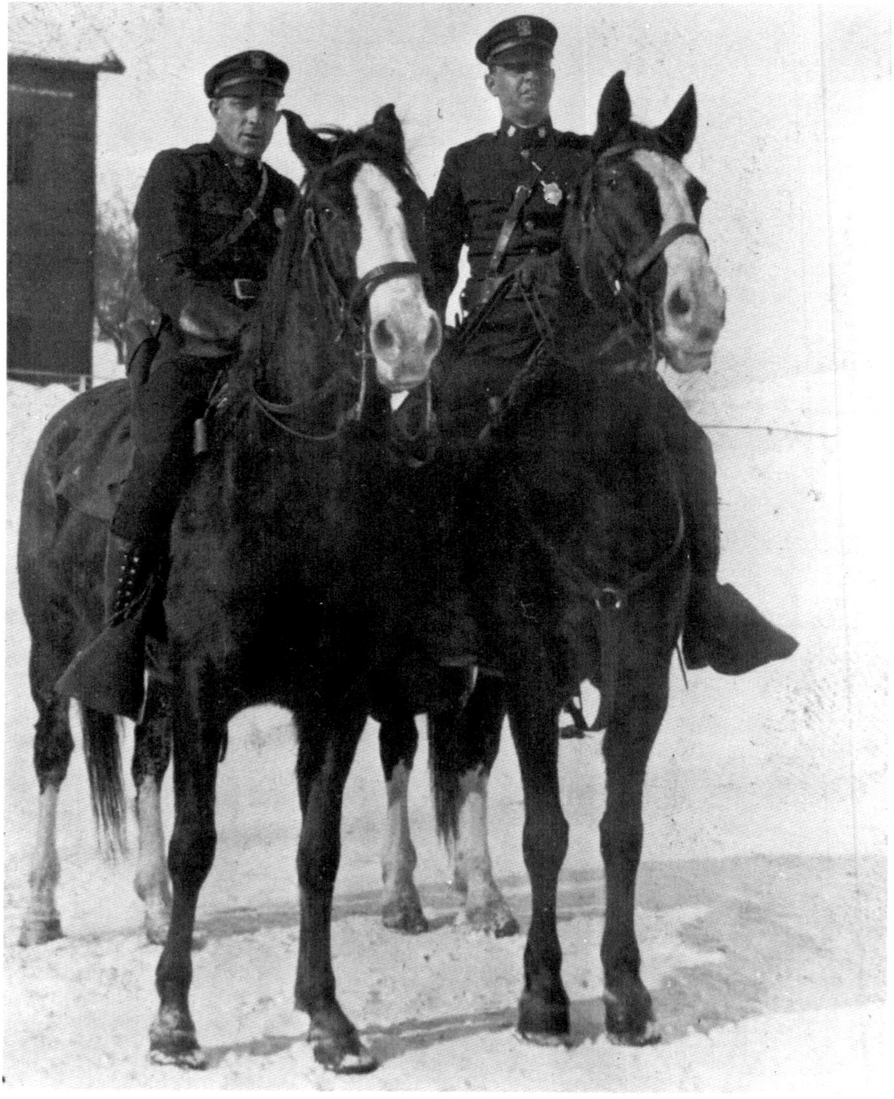

The mounted Michigan Constabulary, later the state police, was established in 1917 and quickly became state enforcers of Prohibition, sometimes referred to as rum hounds. *Courtesy of Superior View.*

barrels of wine, "white mule," bottles filled with "the same kickful material" and half a ton of raisins used to make moonshine. Nineteen officers invaded Delta County, and their raids netted nine arrests. Men from the St. Ignace post made annual raids on the gambling operation at the Grand Hotel—but usually at the end of the season!

Violators did not always interact peacefully during raids conducted by the state police. In late June 1919, Captain Robert E. Marsh and Lieutenant A.D. Vandervort, while on a routine inspection tour of state police posts, left Crystal Falls and encountered a Nash that they suspected of carrying booze. They stopped the car, found ten cases of whiskey, searched the three men for guns and arrested them. The booze and men were loaded in the police car with two deputized youths riding on the running boards. On the way to Bessemer, one of three Croatians sitting in the back of the car, John Davice, pulled out a ".25 calibre vest pocket automatic" from his belt and shot Marsh in the shoulder. Marsh shouted, "I'm paralyzed!" and put the car in neutral. Vandervort, who had his .45-caliber pistol on his lap, instantly killed Davice and grabbed the wheel, putting the car in a ditch. Then he wounded the other two, who tried to escape. Marsh recovered and went on to become the second commander of the state police. Vandervort earned the first Michigan State Police Distinguished Service Citation in 1919 for saving his partner's life.

Some time later, in Escanaba, a twenty-six-year-old bartender, John Kerenski, an employee of Stanley Dobeski, served trooper John M. Sheridan, who entered undercover, a glass of whiskey. Dobeski, who saw this from the end of the bar, yelled, "He's a state policeman! Empty it out! Hit him in the head with the glass!" When Kerenski hurled the glass at Sheridan, the officer opened fire and killed the luckless bartender.

In 1925, five state troopers entered a blind pig in Ishpeming, and a terrible episode occurred. As one of them was seizing moonshine evidence, the bootlegger suddenly opened fire on the troopers, hitting them variously in the shoulders, stomach and feet.

Luckily, the reminiscences of a former trooper, Waino Kokko, have survived and provide insights into the work of one officer. His father, Gus, was a Finnish immigrant and a member of the Negaunee Temperance League, which, at one point, voted to have a man run out of town for selling liquor on Sunday. Yet Gus sold pasties in saloons. Waino grew up with this temperance influence and in 1922, at twenty-two years of age, joined the state police. He spent much of his time tracking down moonshiners and closing speakeasies. As Waino noted, he was involved in countless "whiskey raids and houses of ill fame raids." For him, Sault Ste. Marie was the worst place in the UP for prostitution raids. The major concerns in the copper country were booze and gambling.

Despite the legislative appropriations increasing men and equipment, the commissioner of the Department of Public Safety and the first

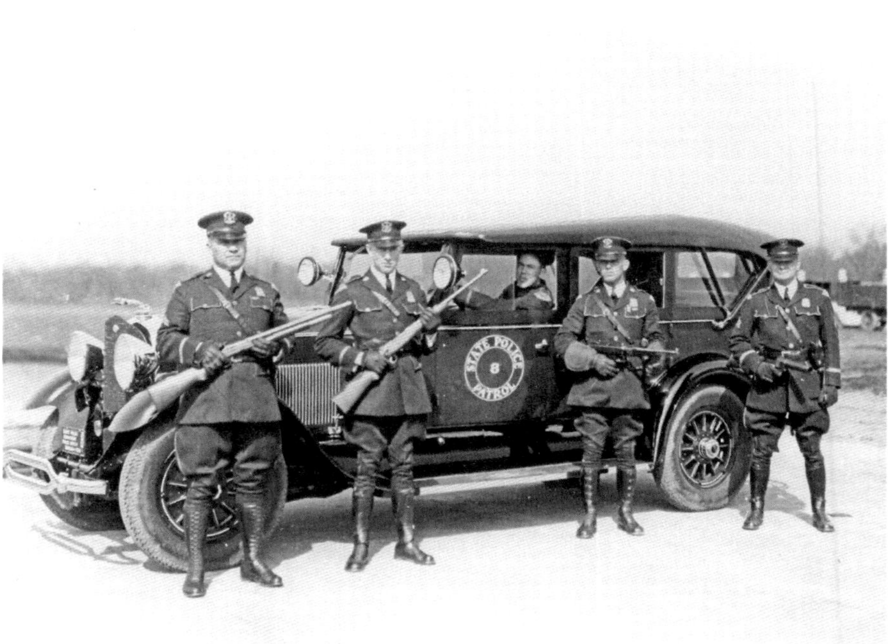

The Michigan State Police were well equipped to take on moonshiners and bootleggers, 1930. *Courtesy of Marquette Regional History Center.*

commander of the state police, Roy C. Vandercook (1873–1958), was questioned about the Prohibition enforcement that he and his officers carried out. In September 1923, he explained his frustrations to a reporter from the *Detroit News*:

> *A man cannot speak with complete understanding of this liquor situation from the office or pulpit. He must ride the roads 24 hours a day in all weather, eat and sleep along the river fronts, push on into shacks and holes where he does not know from one second to next where a shot will come from or careen along the roads at night in a stern chase with the motors roaring and the guns barking. Then he can begin to understand.*

The public did not want the law and did not assist the police in their work. He also found that sheriffs and juries did not do their work and that, when sheriffs did enforce the law, they were voted out of office because they overspent their budgets going after liquor violators. The courts dismissed charges, juries refused to return convictions and superiors withheld money to enforce the law. The unpopular state police were ridiculed by the public.

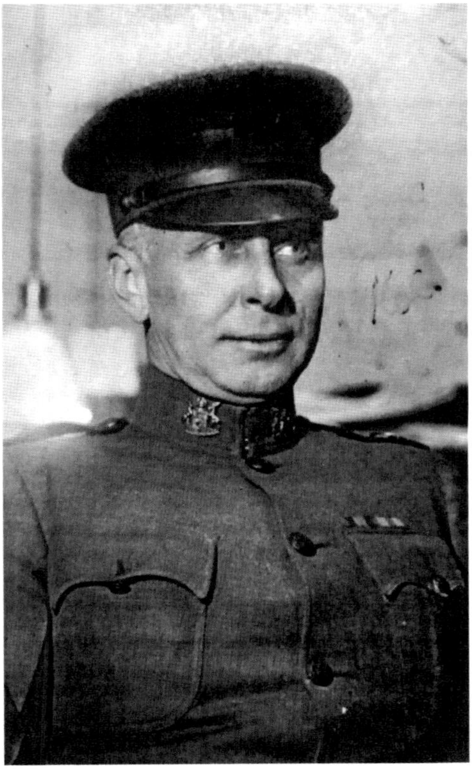

Left: Colonel Roy C. Vandercook, first commander of the Michigan State Police. *Courtesy of R.M. Magnaghi.*

Below: A collection of autos confiscated by the police and agents that were later sold at auction to fund further enforcement efforts. *Courtesy of Marquette Regional History Center.*

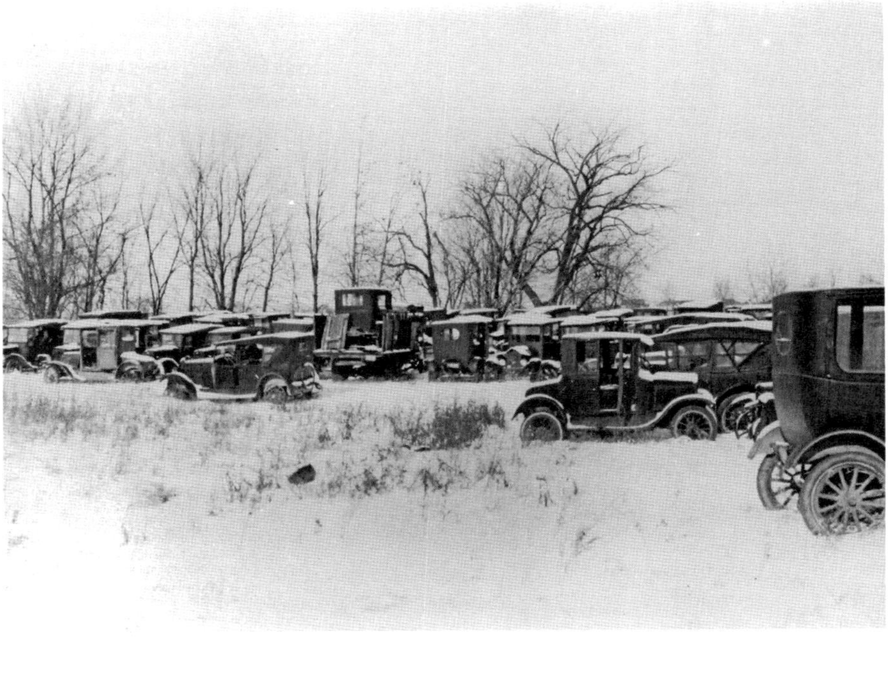

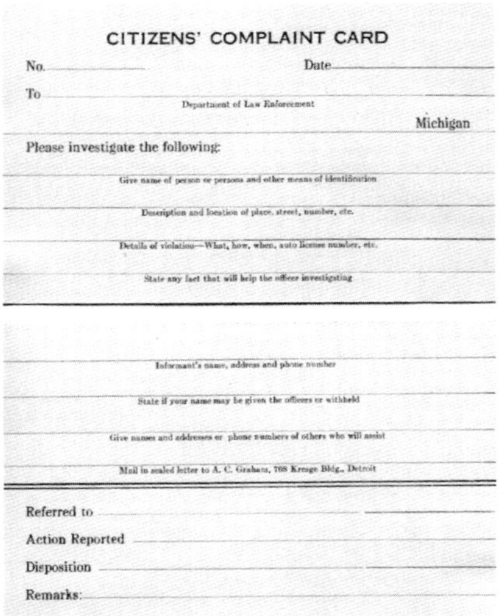

CITIZENS' COMPLAINT CARD

No. ______ Date ______

To ______
Department of Law Enforcement
Michigan

Please investigate the following:

Give name of person or persons and other means of identification

Description and location of place, street, number, etc.

Details of violation—What, how, when, auto license number, etc.

State any fact that will help the officer investigating

Informant's name, address and phone number

State if your name may be given the officers or withheld

Give names and addresses or phone numbers of others who will assist

Mail in sealed letter to A. C. Graham, 708 Kresge Bldg., Detroit

Referred to ______

Action Reported ______

Disposition ______

Remarks: ______

Citizens were encouraged to submit these cards to help police with enforcement. They were generally unsuccessful in the UP. *Courtesy of History & Special Collections, Grand Rapids Public Library.*

Everyone, from rich to poor, violated the law in their own way. Added to all this, the police had to keep long hours and encountered dangerous enforcement situations; in pursuit of bootleggers, some of Vandercook's men were killed, wounded and permanently incapacitated. As a result, many troopers quit while those who remained worked only halfheartedly. Vandercook warned, "We could not enforce the prohibition law in Michigan if we had the United States standing army." He felt that there were areas of the UP that were as bad as Detroit but not as vicious because up north "it is not a commercial proposition with the hijackers, but more of a house consumption business." By the time the article was published, Vandercook was in the process of resigning and got a position as manager and lobbyist with the Michigan Railroad Association.

By the mid-1920s, the Michigan state legislature and Secretary of State Charles J. Deland took the position that the state was not going to appropriate money so that the state police could help federal enforcement agents. The attitude was that Prohibition laws should be enforced like any other law and the state police should not overindulge in going after rumrunners. The monthly report from the Negaunee State Police post showed that forty-eight arrests were made during May 1926 but that only four of them were for liquor violations, which was a dramatic decrease from past statistics. A year later, the *Ironwood Times* added that the state police should not be "spending any undue portion of its time feeling for hip pocket flasks or shaking down mattresses" to the neglect of other duties. Then, in the summer of 1931, the state Supreme Court ruled that a police officer could not randomly slap your hip pocket on suspicion that you were carrying a pint of whiskey in a flask.

SHERIFFS

The next line of enforcement was the county sheriffs, and they accomplished mixed results. State officials did crack down on locations where complaints were the greatest. The attorney general's office had to take action in response to complaints and declared in 1922, "Escanaba... is the Hurley of Michigan. Every soft drink stand is a blind pig, and many saloons flourish in which whiskey and other intoxicating drinks are sold openly across the bar." Gambling went on day and night unmolested by the police. Either in Escanaba or in Delta County, dance halls of the "kind made familiar by the wild west movies flourished unmolested." Naturally, many people who ignored the prohibition law were against the gambling and immorality associated with the dance halls and complained to Attorney General Merlin Wiley. He quickly informed Sheriff Frank O'Dess of the complaints and said he should take immediate action to remedy the situation. Wiley sent an assistant who was accompanied by a member of the state police, and they agreed that the situation was dire. Lumberjacks, railroad laborers, longshoremen and sailors off the ore boats furnished a profitable clientele for bootleggers, rumrunners, professional gamblers and cheap dance hall owners.

Wiley took the position that local county and municipal officials must be on the front line to enforce the law and that they should get the support of the state in the process. As a result, he asked for the immediate resignation of second-term sheriff O'Dess, to which, after some hesitation, O'Dess submitted.

On other occasions, the local sheriffs sat back and took no action. Despite the fact that a notorious pool hall operated in Trenary and readily served liquor to teenagers, the Alger County sheriff did not take action. In the end, federal enforcement agents from Marquette closed the place down.

These unsettled times saw bribes, some of a sexual nature, being made and accepted. In the eastern UP, Oscar Benoit was in state prison for transporting liquor. Deputy Sheriff George Watson of Pickford accosted Benoit's wife, Delie, promising to secure the freedom of her husband for sexual favors. Mrs. Benoit had him return and, in front of two witnesses, repeat the offer, which led to his downfall. In Iron Mountain in 1926, Sheriff Frank Cleveland got his deputies to coax Antonio Bianchetti to make moonshine for them for $70. When the deal was made, Bianchetti was arrested, and the sheriff asked for $1,000 hush money. Bianchetti would only pay $500.

After a lengthy investigation that involved Cleveland's resignation, Deputy Leonard was convicted for giving false testimony and sentenced to three years in federal prison and a $1,000 fine.

The situation involving the county sheriff differed throughout the UP. In Schoolcraft County, Sheriff Jack Hewitt became a legend, enforcing the law and raiding illicit stills. This was also true of the many raids that were recorded in Delta County despite the complaints against O'Dess.

In 1925, it was reported that in Iron Mountain the local police had made only a dozen liquor arrests in the past six years. News stories in the *Ironwood Daily Globe* show that local officials and bootleggers had developed a cozy political alliance based on bribes. As a result, Iron Mountain's "law observance was at the lowest point in any town in the Upper Peninsula."

Soon after, Sheriff Frank Cleveland, Chief of Police Rudolph Freeman and Prosecutor Ray E. MacAllister took action, as reported in the *Iron Mountain News*. In April 1926, Sheriff Cleveland and ten deputies began the process by spending a long night clearing out gambling devices. Then on May 3, "the biggest liquor clean-up in the history of Iron Mountain got underway." Using evidence gathered for two weeks by four private investigators, under total secrecy and financed by Freeman and MacAllister, the police, armed with thirty-four warrants, implemented the heavy hand of the law. Every "joint" on the Midway (three to four blocks of Hughitt Street and Brown Street) was raided. As the paper reported, "The booze emporiums where two-bit moonshine flowed like Niagara Falls saw the river dried up." This was done despite the "spotters" who were ever on guard to report police activity.

Citizens were also concerned with ending prostitution operating under "unparalleled conditions." Young girls with rouged cheeks between sixteen and nineteen years of age were available on the streets for a chance pickup. Older women operated out of brothels. Girls and boys in their teens or barely out of them got drunk and reckless and were admitted without question into bedrooms. Rooms were rented to men seeking a good time who ended being robbed of their wallets.

Conditions that appalled people who had lost hope in the system working were finally exposed. The investigators found a dope ring in operation that eagerly dealt with addicts. Prostitutes were forced out of town or left on their own while spotters maintained a vigil on the prosecutor's office to check on who was reporting to him. Many felt that these vice conditions had been attracted by the boom created by the development of Ford's auto plant in neighboring Kingsford.

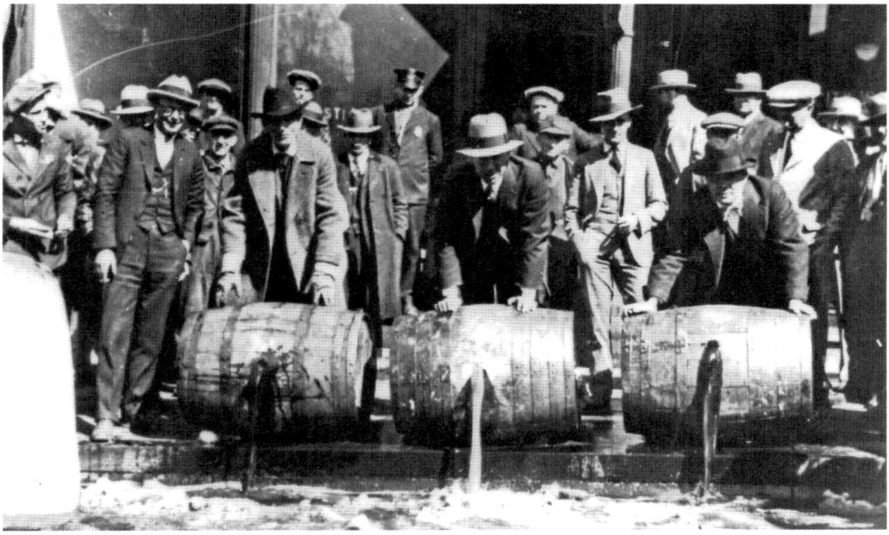

Above: After a major raid at Iron Mountain in 1926, Federal Prohibition Enforcement agents poured gallons of wine into the sewer. *Courtesy of Marquette Regional History Center.*

Below: Tough economic times caused some women to turn to prostitution. *Courtesy Superior of View.*

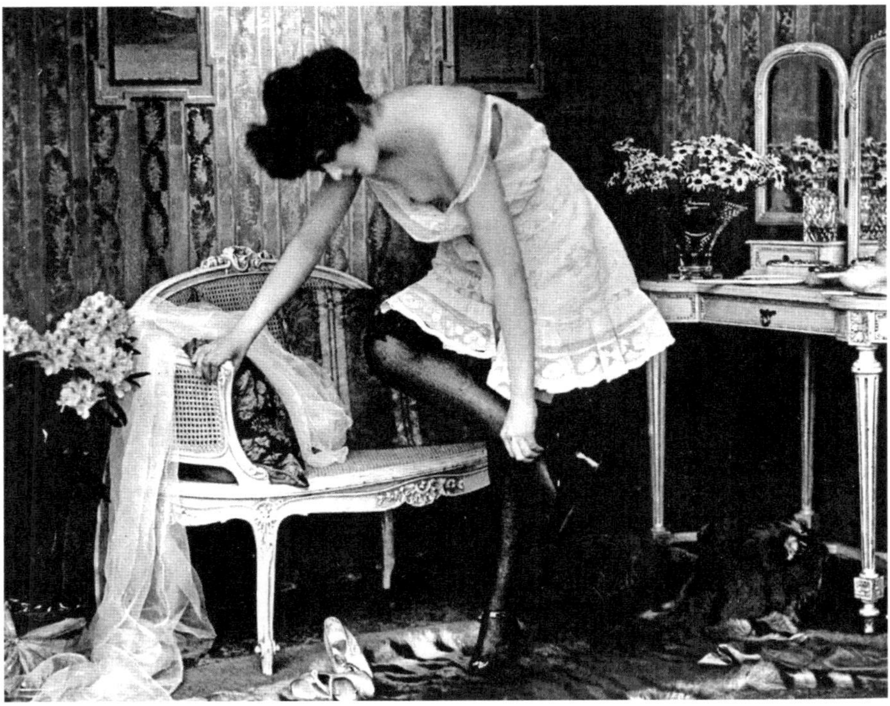

Due to these raids, the police and public learned more details about how the Midway joints operated. The booze supply was hidden behind sliding panels in chimneys and walls, in secret compartments in lavatories, under trapdoors, in backyard recesses, in back of pans and kettles and, in one case, in a neighboring barbershop. Coffee pots, pitchers and bottles were favorite receptacles that could be easily dumped or broken in a raid. Moonshine came in two grades: the good and the not-so-good. The latter was "almost powerful enough to melt the glass" and was the most coveted because of its cheap price. The moonshine was not produced in Iron Mountain but in Wisconsin, and through a system of flashing warning lights, was driven into Iron Mountain.

The rum row fraternity made a great deal of money through gambling. Customers entered these basement gambling dens through side and hidden doors, down stairs and through a labyrinth of corridors and rooms. Blackjack, poker and craps were the most popular games. The stakes were as high as one wanted to go.

CITY POLICE

On the community level, police enforcement varied. In Marquette during the 1920s, the chief of police's annual reports show large numbers of people arrested for drunkenness or driving drunk, but two or three arrested for violating the Volstead Act. Some of the chiefs enjoyed poker and drinks at private homes. In some instances, speakeasies existed close to the police stations or enforcement headquarters. In Marquette, a speakeasy operated across the street from the federal building while in Menominee the police station shared a building that also housed a speakeasy.

The UP Firemen's Association had its annual tournament in Negaunee in July 1921. The city authorities intimated to Captain A.A. Downing of the state police that for the sake of hospitality, they should ignore the liquor violations. Dowling reported that "some of the most industrious and best rewarded peddlers of shine were members of the squad of special officers sworn to enforce the law." Because of the sale of moonshine and drunkenness, the event turned into an "orgy." In response to this, George Newett, editor of the *Ishpeming Iron Ore*, decried the event. He noted that it was "a mistake to defy a law calculated for the correct morals of people" and thus set a bad example for the youth, who should be kept out of the

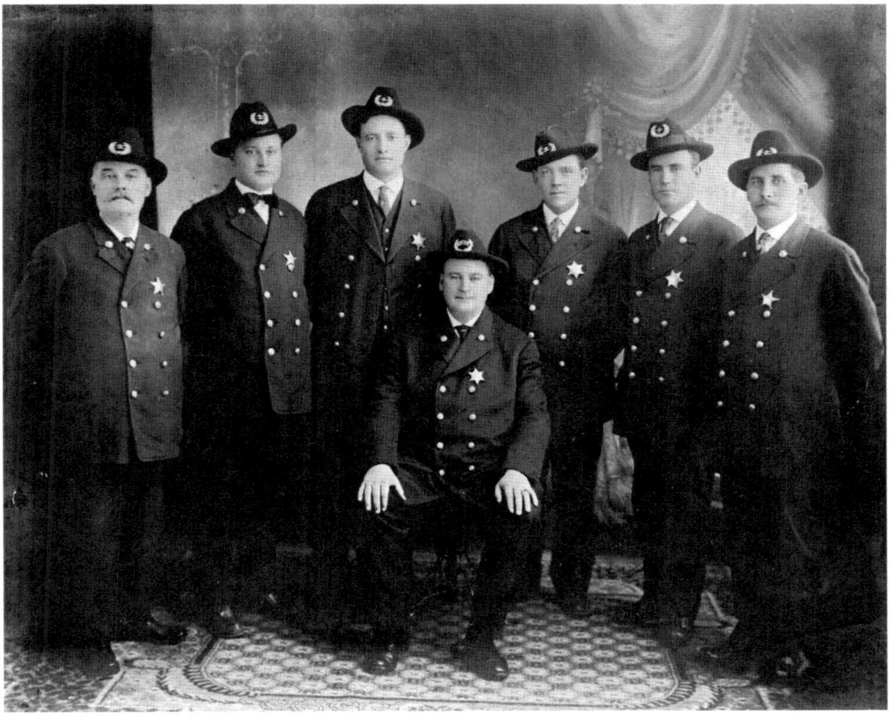

The local police, seen here in Negaunee, Michigan, were supposed to play a major enforcement role but, in general, "looked the other way." *Courtesy of Superior View.*

path of temptation. Finally the "unchallenged presence of liquor reflects upon the state police."

The stories of bribing police and everyone involved with handling moonshine are legend. Bribes became an important part of life in the 1920s and early 1930s. Charles Stakel, who was in charge of the YMCA in Marquette, said that the Y always got funded. The town marshal Jack Lacey shook down speakeasy owners for $1,000 annually and gave the money to the YMCA. The highways from Hurley, the entry point for Canadian liquor to Milwaukee and Chicago, had to be free to hijackers, and the police were paid to look the "look the other way" or stop the hijackers. An alliance developed between the bootleggers and the authorities that led to Iron Mountain being considered the worst center of crime in the UP in 1926.

The profits were big, and the enforcers were poorly paid. As the editor and reporters for the *Ironwood Times* and other newspapers on the eve of repeal noted, the enforcement of Prohibition in the UP could be classified as nil. It was the hypocritical farce that many had said it would be.

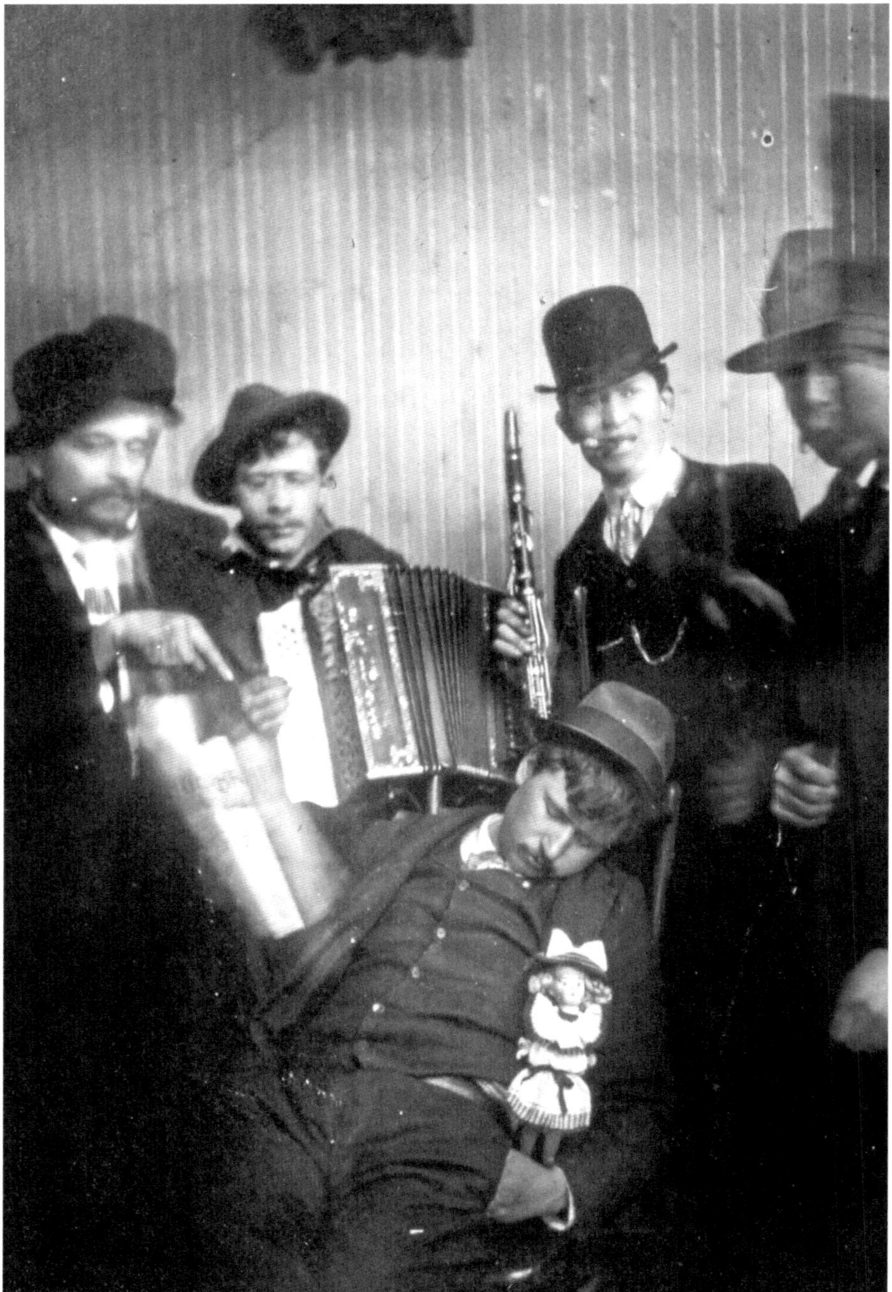

Prohibition ended the convivial nature of saloons, and many people entered a speakeasy to quickly get drunk in case there was a raid. *Courtesy of R.M. Magnaghi.*

RUMRUNNING

With the reality of Prohibition, Michigan's lengthy border with Canada made its narrow points on the border ideal for rumrunning. There are three areas where narrow rivers—the Detroit, St. Clair and St. Mary's—allowed the swift and easy passage of liquor into the United States. The best known of these crossings is between Detroit and Windsor, where it has been estimated that between 75 and 85 percent of all the liquor that entered the United States passed. Some fifty miles to the north through Lake St. Clair and the St. Clair is Port Huron and its Canadian sister, Sarnia. The last of these borders was on the St. Mary's River, which divided Sault Ste. Marie, Michigan and Ontario. This latter border area is more than the constricted river but subsequently flows into a labyrinth of islands and channels to the southeast, making enforcement a nightmare. In the North Country, beside the Sault Ste. Marie entry point, you faced upper Lake Huron and the North Channel and the vast expanse of Lake Superior with Canadian fishing villages and the port-rail cities of Fort William and Port Arthur (modern Thunder Bay).

Historians have ignored these latter routes because they are far from populated areas and the more obvious markets for illegal Canadian and British liquor. On the Canadian side of the border, provincial prohibition went into effect on September 1, 1916, and ended in 1927. In Ontario, the sale of alcoholic beverages, either in bars or for home consumption, was outlawed, but the new law did not prevent the import and export of alcohol. Furthermore, the Canadians felt that enforcement of the American law was not their concern. With the start of Michigan prohibition on May 1, 1918, the Canadians had their market across the border.

Liquor that landed on either coast was transported across Canada along the Canadian Pacific Railway. To further facilitate the transport and marketing of liquor was the Bronfman family in Canada. They arrived in Canada in the 1880s as immigrants from Romania. They quickly left their Saskatchewan farm and became major bootleggers and later distillers, supplying the Capone gang of Chicago, the notorious Purple Gang of Detroit and smaller operations.

The liquor trade included Scotch whiskey, bourbon, rye, gin, champagne and liqueurs—all quality products—but not moonshine. In 1927, one shipment of 340 cases was valued at $12,150 (that's $165,432 in 2016 dollars), and another one of 565 cases cost $20,180 ($274,768 today). This made smuggling a valuable enterprise and worth the risk.

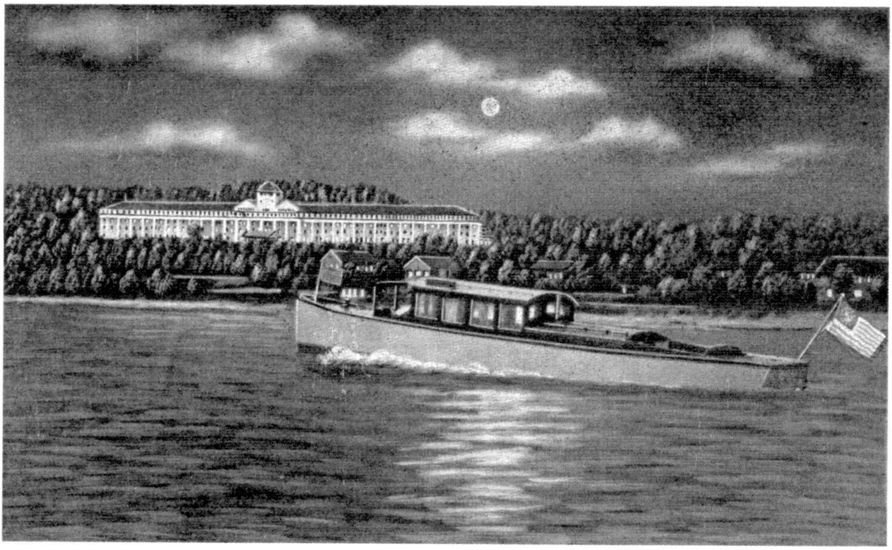

Fast motorboats plied the waters between the Grand Hotel and Canada, bringing in cases of Canadian and British liquor. *Courtesy of Mackinac Island State Park.*

An article in the *Soo Evening News* in July 1926 indicated that the amounts of liquor that were imported to the Canadian Soo went as high as $50,000 and $100,000 ($669,254 and $1.3 million in 2016 dollars) and involved "big money," possibly with international connections since local people could not finance such an operation. Small launches took the liquor cargo to tramp steamers that sailed to lower lake urban centers, where the demand was greatest. Liquor was landed at isolated locations on the St. Mary's River and trucked to Chicago or returned to dry Ontario.

There were major markets in the urban centers of the Midwest—Detroit, Chicago and Milwaukee. However, the Upper Peninsula was a liquor transfer point and destination, especially for the many resorts located on the peninsula, in neighboring northwest Michigan, on the Door Peninsula in Wisconsin and in northern Wisconsin. The upscale resort country in the Upper Peninsula was concentrated in the eastern part of the region in the Les Cheneaux Islands at the mouth of the St. Mary's River and at Mackinac Island, dominated by the Grand Hotel a mere forty miles to the west. Northwest Michigan from Harbor Springs, across Little Traverse Bay to Petoskey and Charlevoix and south to Traverse City, was another important resort area that developed in the late nineteenth century. Across Lake Michigan is the Door Peninsula and northern Wisconsin, which attracted more affluent midwesterners from Chicago and Milwaukee. These resorters were in the market for fine food and imported liquor from Canada and Britain and not the local moonshine of questionable quality and taste.

With Sault Ste. Marie as liquor headquarters and money to be made, the results could be anticipated. It was difficult for Canadian officials to control liquor seizures in late 1925. Canadian authorities seized a quantity of liquor and stored it in the courthouse, but some of the confiscated amount was stolen. The Consolidated Exporters Association of Vancouver, British Columbia, maintained an agent at Sault Ste. Marie whose primary business was to smuggle booze into the United States through the porous border. Joseph Hobbs, a former resident of Sault Ste. Marie, returned home as a representative of an unnamed "Scotch whiskey company." On July 9, 1927, the *St. Ignace Republican News* reported that conditions were out of control given the amount of liquor being shipped through Sault Ste. Marie and "hi-jacking and warfare between bootlegging factions is momentarily expected."

During this time, an American consular office operated out of the Canadian Soo, and following a December 11, 1924 directive, reports relating to Prohibition were sent to the State Department on a regular basis, especially during 1925–27. Unfortunately, these reports by Herbert W. Carlson and Bartley F. Yost do not provide much information on the quantity of booze being shipped across the border but show how porous the Soo border was. Canadian authorities were supposed to notify U.S. Customs of an export shipment, but in many cases, the notification came after the fact. The consular reports show that liquor cleared Canada and was shipped out in tonnage from tramp steamers and good-sized river craft to speedboats and fourteen-foot skiffs. A small operation conducted by two Canadians working with Samuel Banker of Chicago tried to smuggle twenty cases of champagne across the St. Mary's River in December 1929 but were caught at the Union Carbide plant.

Shipments of liquor were trucked to locations away from the Soo: northwest to Batchawana Bay and other locations on Lake Superior and downriver from Sault Ste. Marie to Sugar Island and Kensington Point. Flashing lights alerted bootleggers on the American side of a run from Batchawana Bay, and liquor arrived at Whitefish Point, where gangs awaited the arrival, loaded it into Whiskey Sixes and headed for Chicago. Al Capone was known to maintain a fast speedboat, *Norco*, at this location.

There were some rather unique smuggling operations, such as the three Italians from Negaunee who went to the Canadian Soo and bought several burlap sacks filled with bottled liquor. They hired a boat and crossed into

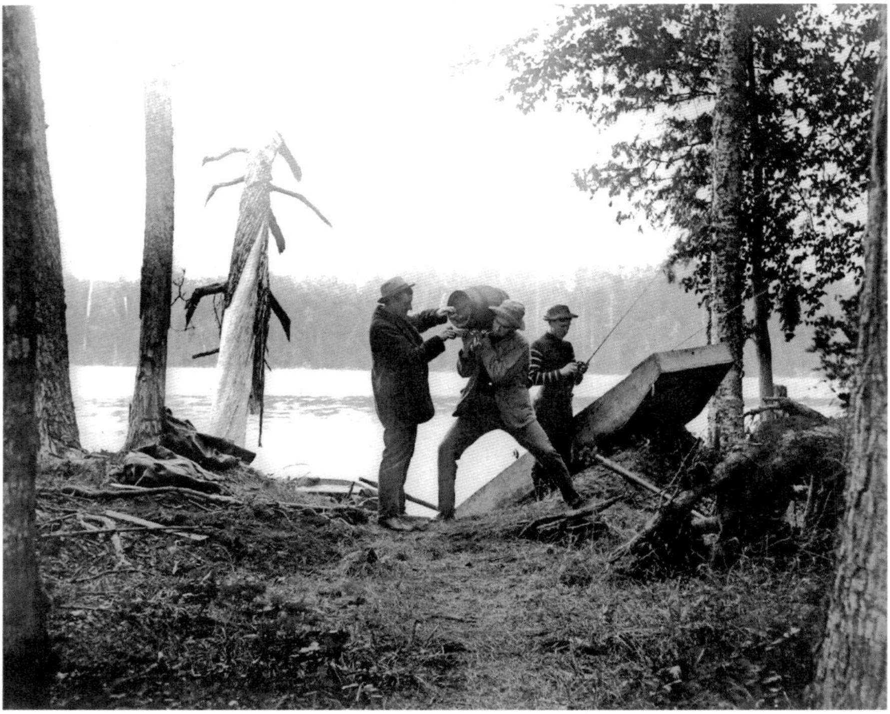

Canadian booze was unloaded at Whitefish Point and shipped to Chicago. *Courtesy of Superior View.*

the United States and then had the boat take them along the desolate southern shore of Lake Superior. At Grand Marais, they buried the cache in the sand until the third member returned from Negaunee with a truck to haul it home. In the process, they attracted attention in the town, and the Coast Guard lighthouse keeper got wind of their operation and had them arrested.

The two Saults were an easy and obvious point of crossing for liquor into the United States. However, there were other, lengthier routes across Lake Superior from Port Arthur (now Thunder Bay) and through North Channel, part of Lake Huron.

The distance across Lake Superior made it easy for rumrunners to lose patrol boats, both lacking radar and efficient communication. The major Canadian outlet in western Lake Superior was Port Arthur located on the Canadian Pacific Railway. Here Allan Bronfman owned and operated the Martiaggi Hotel, which was considered a staging area for liquor to be shipped across Lake Superior. Even tiny fishing and coaling towns like Jaw Fish along the line had access to whiskey and beer made in a production center like Waterloo, Ontario, or imported through Vancouver already distilled.

Liquor from Port Arthur easily found its way to the resorts of Isle Royale, which is twenty miles at its closest to the Canadian border. Maritime historian Fred Stonehouse relates a story from the 1970s when he and associates were diving shipwrecks. One day, Lake Superior was too rough for diving so the divers anchored their boat in a protected cove. While waiting for the weather to clear, Fred dove the site and found the bottom lined with bottles obviously from a rumrunner wreck.

For rumrunners, the big money was to be made getting liquor to urban centers like Duluth, Superior and Ashland. In the UP, north of Ironwood-Hurley is Little Girls Point, an example of a landing spot along the isolated Lake Superior coast. In July 1920, the first shipment of liquor arrived. It consisted of 2,220 cases of fine Johnnie Walker Scotch valued at $19,980 (about $236,679 today). On arrival, it was loaded and trucked the dozen miles to Ironwood, where the "inner gossip" told of several well-known Ironwood people declaring they purchased some of the shipment and placed it in their booze cellars. Then the shipment went to Hurley for local use and resorts, but the bulk of the Scotch went to Milwaukee and Chicago. This remote landing was an easily accessible border gateway to interior markets.

Canadian whiskey arrived by not only boat but also seaplane. One story is told that Capone had seaplanes with liquor land on a lake near his vacation home near Hayward, Wisconsin. Ed Soderberg, in his twenties and a veteran of World War I, started his career as a barnstorming pilot. Seeing the adventure and profitability in aerial rumrunning, he flew liquor from Canada into northern Wisconsin and the Upper Peninsula.

Fishermen at desolate locations like Jaw Fish were willing to run liquor across Lake Superior for a fee of $600 (about $8,173 today). Rumrunners landed the illicit cargo in Marquette at the foot of Baraga Avenue, stored it in a waterside building and sold it from there. Rum Runners Cove was located several miles northwest of Marquette. In eastern Lake Superior, liquor was run from Batchawana Bay to Whitefish Point. One story tells of Al Capone operating the *Norco*, which made the run, and then the liquor was trucked to Chicago. Canadian Customs officials became concerned with this route because returning smugglers brought silks and other textiles into Canada.

NORTH CHANNEL, ONTARIO

To historians and the general public, North Channel at the northern end of Lake Huron was a little-known gateway for Canadian liquor to enter the United States. Gangsters and operatives from Chicago, Milwaukee and elsewhere, however, were well aware of this border gateway.

Towns on the North Channel—Blind River and Thessalon—were also on the railway and points of export. Boats traveled twenty-five miles or fewer to enter U.S. waters and then easily could elude the Coast Guard or minimal federal agents in the channels and islands of the St. Mary's River. Canadian St. Joseph Island, an entry point on the river, is a mere five hundred feet from the U.S. shore. Hilton Beach on the east side of the island was a staging area for booze shipments, and as a matter of fact, a Mr. Falby from Chicago owned a hotel-transfer spot here. At one point, the Coast Guard kept a cutter, *Vigilant*, in the vicinity because of the known traffic. The other staging area was Mackinac Island, where agents for the Purple Gang and the Capone syndicate organized shipments and transferred them to ships for the voyage south.

There were many connections between men in Blind River, Sugar Island and Sault Ste. Marie and men from Chicago and Milwaukee. In 1929, as rumrunning on the Detroit River was tightened up by the dry navy, attention was turned north. On August 23, 1929, the yacht *Dryad* was intercepted in the Straits of Mackinac by the Coast Guard. It had been loaded at Blind River with 500 cases of Canadian Soo–brewed ale and beer. The crew had dumped 450 cases into the lake, so federal agents retrieved only 50 from the yacht. Carl Lindburg, a farmer on Sugar Island, worked with three Milwaukee men to smuggle liquor across the narrow channel between the island and Canada.

Channel boats carried liquor across Mississagi Strait to Cockburn Island and the western end of Manitoulin Island. At the former, it was a quick run to Drummond Island in the United States, or they used small Greene Island to the southeast to await the arrival of large vessels to carry the liquor to urban centers.

Not all of the liquor that flowed across the border traveled out of the area. Fast Chris Craft and Hacker Craft wooden motorboats painted black carried the liquor to northern Michigan. Beginning in the 1890s, the area became the summer destination for affluent midwesterners, including the Swifts, Armours, Wrigleys, Gambles (of Procter & Gamble), Fords and Wilsons (of General Motors). Trains brought them north from Chicago, Detroit, Cincinnati, Cleveland and St. Louis.

In the eastern Upper Peninsula, the Les Cheneaux Island and Mackinac Island became major resort centers. The Grand Hotel on Mackinac Island, a monument to the Victorian era, was built in 1887. Given its scenic location in the Straits of Mackinac, wealthy vacationers traveled north by ship or rail to enjoy its cool climate, scenery and the fine liquor and gambling that were readily available.

In an attempt to provide something "different" for summer visitors, Herb Pfeiffelman and his father, Walter, bought the *Flying Spray*, *Let's Go*, *Fleetwood 1* and *Fleetwood 2* from Hacker Craft while the Arnold line matched their service with two Chris Craft, *Frances K* and *Good News*, which made fast and exhilarating trips around the island in twenty-five minutes and had regular and charter trips to Mackinaw City, Cheboygan and St. Ignace. The world's first Chris Craft distributor, E.J. Mertaugh Boat Works, was established in 1925 and is located in Hessel in the heart of the Les Cheneaux archipelago.

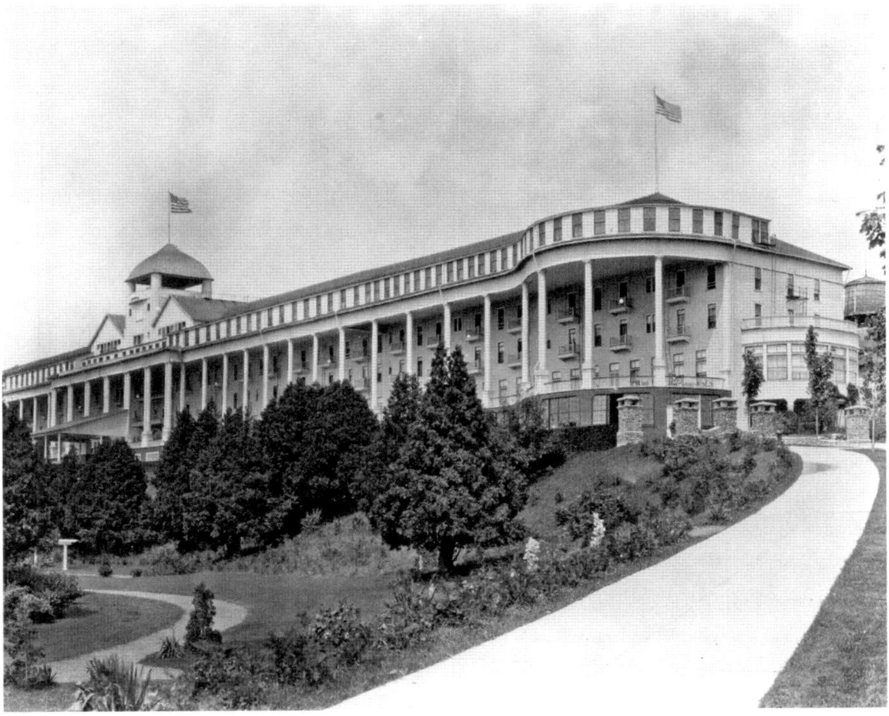

The Grand Hotel was the center of 1920s tourism and home to fine food, drink and gambling. *Courtesy of Mackinac Island State Park.*

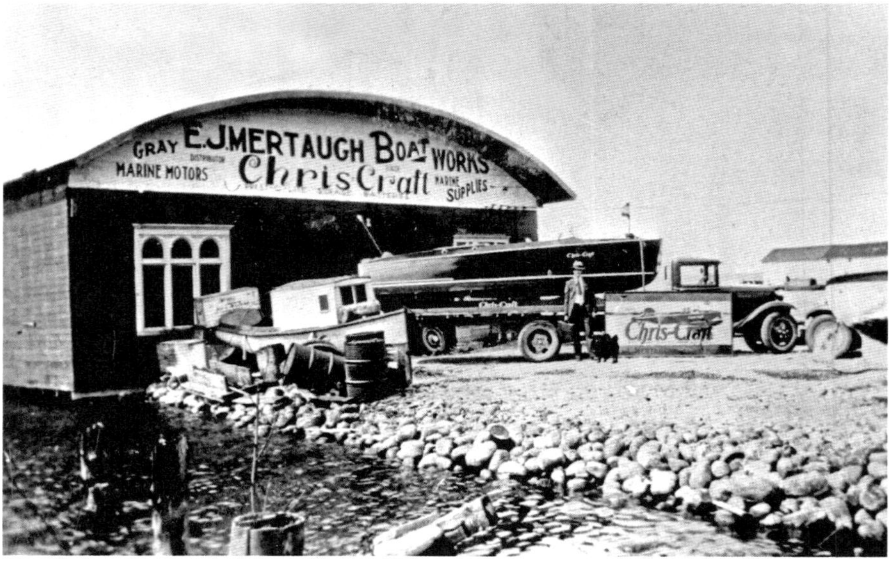

The E.J. Mertaugh Boat Works at Hessel provided early Chris Craft to the eastern UP. *Courtesy of Superior View.*

Did these fast speedboats remain at the dock during the night hours? There was money to be made rumrunning to nearby Canada. Edward "Ned" Fenlon, born in 1903, grew up in Hessel and became a lawyer, state representative and circuit judge. During the 1920s, when he was a student at Notre Dame University and needed tuition money, he delivered newspapers and elite guests to the Grand Hotel. However, at night, he became involved in what was called "international trade," bringing Canadian whiskey to Mackinac. Then there were yachtsmen who spent time in Canada and returned with liquor hidden under the floorboards of their yachts. A regular route developed to supply Lower Michigan. It ran down the St. Mary's River to Nun's Creek, where it was stored for the night. Then it was run across the Straits of Mackinac to the Cheboygan River and Duncan Bay in the vicinity of Cheboygan to be picked up for land transit southward. One fellow, fearing arrest, dumped twenty-five to thirty cases of liquor into the lake, which was an expensive evasion. Boats from Chicago brought liquor that was quietly sold by crew vendors to local retail liquor outlets on Mackinac. You always had to be careful that you were purchasing actual liquor. Dr. Guy Bailey made contact with a vendor on a Great Lakes cruise ship and bought three fifths of whiskey for twenty-five dollars only to find out that the fifths were filled with cold tea. Summer cottagers also brought their own liquor from Chicago and Detroit, at first unsure of the local supply.

Some thirty miles to the southwest of Mackinac was the resort area of northwestern Michigan running from Harbor Springs through Petoskey and Charlevoix to Grand Traverse Bay and Traverse City. Frequent rail service brought thousands of affluent vacationers. The most famous casino to open in Harbor Springs was the Club Manitou. Abe Bernstein, a frequent visitor who loved the area and leader of the Purple Gang, decided to open the club in 1929. He saw that wealthy people wanted fine food, imported liquor, dancing, entertainment and gambling. In the heavily guarded basement, alcohol, slot machines, roulette tables, barcarole and poker tables were available. A strict policy kept locals out of the club but provided jobs. Bribes to local officials kept the club opened until the early 1950s. Due to Club Manitou and other casinos, rumrunners from Canada had a ready market for their goods.

Other rumrunners went west directly across Lake Michigan and brought liquor to the resorts on the Door Peninsula of Wisconsin that attracted vacationers from Milwaukee and Chicago. To the west in northern Wisconsin, there was another set of resort towns that attracted a similar clientele, among them Al Capone and his rival Roger Tuohy, who fished with a machine gun at his side. Liquor was shipped north from Chicago and Milwaukee by Whiskey Sixes and by water to Green Bay. The *Ironwood Times* at the end of August 1920 was concerned about a shootout that had taken place between Bessemer and Ironwood and strongly urged rumrunners to use Wisconsin roads exclusively if they were traveling between Green Bay and Hurley.

The UP was the gateway for this booze traffic that poured into the area and beyond. There was also a vacationers' market in the Upper Peninsula that since the advent of the automobile had been attracting tourists. During the 1920s, hotels, campgrounds, private homes and the emerging motels were filled with visitors who wanted to quench their thirst. Given the proximity of the Keweenaw Peninsula to Canada, many individuals ran liquor to fill the demand.

Compared to the Atlantic coast, there are few accounts of rumrunners and their capture on the northern Great Lakes, but the following four accounts are insightful. The ships involved are the *Arbutus* in 1920–21, the *Oscar Newmen* in 1927, the *Geronimo* in 1928 and 1930 and the *Faithful* in 1928.

ODYSSEY OF THE *ARBUTUS*

The *Arbutus* was a sixty-three-foot wooden-hull Canadian-owned tug built thirty-three years earlier. Rumrunners liked older boats because if they were seized or had to be scuttled, the loss was minimal. In mid-November 1920, the *Arbutus*, commanded by Captain George Stitt, sailed from Port Arthur with a cargo of seventy cases of liquor consigned to a Houghton man. On the voyage across Lake Superior, the captain and his crew decided to imbibe some of their cargo and accidentally landed at Copper Harbor. On the morning of November 20, the lighthouse keeper, Charles T. Davis, rowed over to the *Arbutus* and learned from one of the crew that they were carrying "a lot of wet goods"—twenty-two cases of Scotch and forty-eight cases of rye. Realizing that this was a rumrunner, Davis drove the dozen miles to Delaware, where he called the collector of customs at Hancock and alerted him of the smuggled goods.

At 10:45 a.m., the *Arbutus* weighed anchor and headed southward toward Houghton, its destination. However, the tug, having exhausted its coal supply and in heavy seas, was forced to seek shelter at Eagle Harbor. Captain Stitt anchored the tug in the harbor and warned that enforcement agents were on the way to seize the tug and its crew. Captain Stitt abandoned the crew and fled with a copper country resident to Houghton. There they got a room, where Stitt originally registered using his own name but, apparently as an afterthought, erased the name and wrote "George Phillips, Duluth." But the "Capt. Stitt" he wrote first was still plainly visible. By the next morning, they were nowhere in sight, having left on a morning train, probably heading toward Sault Ste. Marie because authorities at Duluth had been warned to watch for them.

Meanwhile, almost as soon as the tug anchored, complications arose for law enforcement. The presence of the tug in Eagle Harbor placed it under the jurisdiction of Keweenaw County officials, but there were two problems. The tug was not docked but anchored in the harbor, and thus, county officials could take no action. Furthermore, since it was Canadian owned, there were international complications that would have to be handled by the federal government. Without any direction, county officials sat and waited while the captain and crew fled.

Now the federal government took action. Chief enforcement agent Leo J. Grove in Marquette sent his most qualified agent, John Saul, to Eagle Harbor to take over the investigation. As the hours passed, action finally took place. Saul, prosecuting attorney of Keweenaw County Nels A. Ruonavaara,

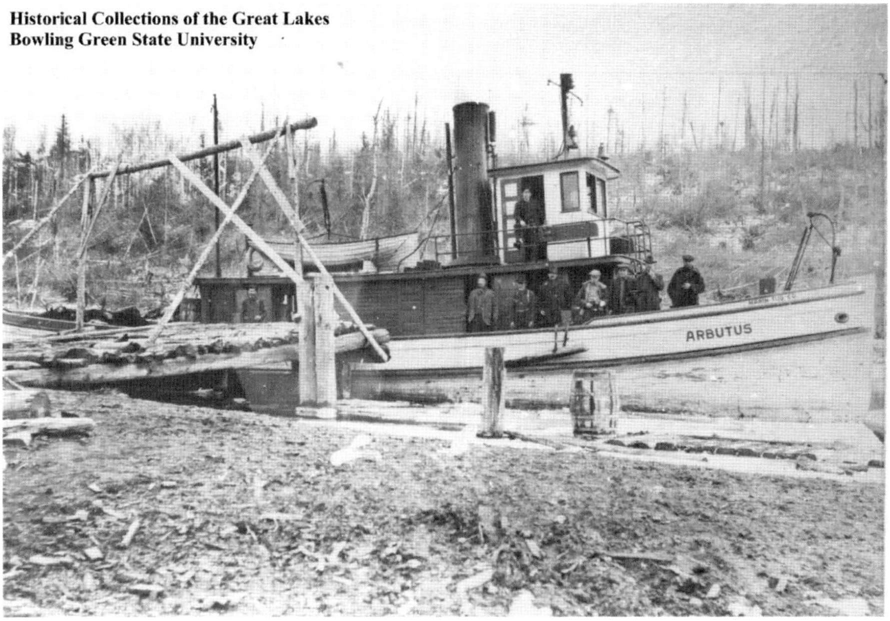

The ill-fated *Arbutus*. *Courtesy Historical Center of the Great Lakes, Bowling Green State University.*

Undersheriff Heikkila and Deputy Sheriff Roy Trudell headed for Eagle Harbor. The first to fall was John Dowd, a passenger on the tug and the shipper of the liquor. He was arrested on the evening of November 23, arraigned by Justice Richards of Mohawk and placed in the county jail at Eagle River.

That afternoon, Saul and the collector of customs hired a small boat and were taken to the tug. When they boarded the vessel, they found only engineer James Dampier, who remained on board because the vessel could be seized by anyone if left abandoned. According to his sworn testimony, the *Arbutus* sailed from Port Arthur with thirty cases of illegal whiskey, although later the number rose to seventy cases. Dampier said once the captain fled and before the tug was to be seized, he decided to throw the remaining twenty-one cases of liquor overboard.

As with many enforcement actions during Prohibition, the law was vague, especially in this case. Saul concluded to a reporter after he had seized the tug, "I am not sure what I will do next." He sent a full report of the seizure to enforcement officials in Chicago and Grand Rapids and awaited a reply. The report stated that John Dowd, who had been arrested, owned the liquor and that Captain Stitt knew the liquor was on board. According to licenses found on board, Samuel Wright of Fort William owned the vessel.

A diver was hired, and men with grappling hooks unsuccessfully searched the twenty-foot-deep waters. What Dampier did not say was that when he threw the liquor over board, someone in a motorboat alongside had retrieved it, brought it to shore and sold the liquor. Dowd, held in the county jail, made a written confession to the prosecutor. Federal district attorney M.H. Walker informed county officials that federal warrants for transporting liquor were issued for both Dowd and Dampier. However, Walker wanted the investigation expanded. The *Mining Journal* reporter wrote that this action "may result in the implication of several persons, some of them prominent in the copper country, on charges of smuggling and conspiracy against the government." Federal officials claimed that they had evidence that the liquor was consigned to Houghton people and that they held a telegram with pertinent information they did not share with the media.

The federal government said that the vessel was worth between $4,000 and $5,000, and according to federal statutes, it could be released if its owners furnished bonds for double its value. Canadian interests who held mortgages on the tug hired a copper country attorney to deal with the legal implications. Matters became even more complicated. Grove received information that persons holding mortgages on the tug were not inclined to furnish bonds for its release because, in the event of its sale, the court would have to recognize the lien of the mortgage holders.

The reporter concluded that it might turn out that the vessel will be a "white elephant" on the hands of federal agents. The tug was reported leaky and not in good condition. The federal agents did not know what to do with the tug if it was not released. A licensed pilot would have to be hired to bring the tug to Marquette.

Saul was a confident and diligent federal enforcement agent. He quickly concluded that Dampier had unloaded the liquor and found unmistakable signs on shore that a small boat had landed the cargo, which was dragged up on shore and loaded into one or more automobiles. He unearthed clues as to the whereabouts of the whiskey, and these clues led to finding some of the liquor and, in the process, gathering confessions from people. The agents were more interested in "higher ups" involved in the smuggling process. He found that Dowd was merely the transport agent and not the purchaser. Saul was actually seeking the purchaser and the distributors. Dampier had been instructed to unload the liquor and then burn the *Arbutus*.

The tug, now referred to as "the booze ship," finally loaded with coal sailed for Houghton and arrived on December 3. The tug was to continue to Marquette. However, a check of its condition worried Captain Thomas Brown of Munising, and he was afraid to venture onto Lake Superior until the fog lifted. A check of the vessel showed that the ship's compass had been broken during the excitement of the seizure, the original crew and captain familiar with the vessel were gone and the tug was reported to be leaking.

When conditions improved, Captain Brown headed the tug for Marquette, and federal agent Joseph Pavlok oversaw the voyage. The tug made it to Marquette and was winterized at the Coast Guard station there. The Canadian owners of the tug convinced federal authorities that they were ignorant of the boat's mission to American waters, and so it was returned.

The saga of the *Arbutus* did not end in Marquette. In November 1921, the tug continued its odyssey on Lake Superior. It left Marquette and headed for Sault Ste. Marie. Due to heavy seas, the *Arbutus* foundered some fifteen miles northeast of Grand Marais, Michigan. The Coast Guard rescued its crew, which consisted of Captain E.A. Fader of Fort William, William Toms of Port Arthur, engineer J.A. Ranger and Albert Qilliam of Marquette. Can divers visit the hulk? This is not an option, as this is one of the deepest areas of the lake.

The story could continue, with the legal cases of a number of copper country people who were tried in federal court at Sault Ste. Marie. Most of them got $500 fines for their involvement in this rumrunning venture.

As mentioned, this is one of the few examples of a rumrunner being intercepted by federal enforcement agents, mainly due to bad judgment on the part of the shippers in Port Arthur and the captain. It also shows how the Prohibition enforcement directives were difficult to administer, although due to the persistence of John Saul, violators were apprehended and got their day in court.

Oscar Newman's Quiet End

This two-masted schooner was built in 1876 and served the logging industry before working in northern Lake Michigan ports carrying mundane cargoes of flour and vinegar. Around 1910, the schooner was given a gasoline engine, and a few years later, the masts were removed. Its venture into rumrunning is little chronicled. On July 7, 1927, the *Oscar Newman* with its crew of three was stranded off Rocky Point at Mud Lake, a traditional transfer point for liquor along the St. Mary's River. An accidental fire destroyed the aged vessel.

GERONIMO'S EXCITING CAREER

There are few detailed stories of ships that were stopped and seized by the Coast Guard in the northern Great Lakes. On May 19, 1928, the 150-foot *Geronimo*, a former tender for the Canadian lighthouse service, departed Windsor, Ontario. It was heavily loaded with four thousand cases of liquor valued at $250,000 ($3.4 million in today's dollars) with Chicago as its destination. The Internal Revenue Service at Sault Ste. Marie was informed of the *Geronimo* and its illicit cargo. The Coast Guard cutter *Cook* and the *CG-118* were dispatched from the Soo to Detour, at the mouth of the St. Mary's River, with sealed orders to intercept the *Geronimo*. This was done so that no one could send out a warning. In the early hours of Monday, May 21, they intercepted the *Geronimo* in the Straits four and a half miles northwest of Mackinaw City. In an attempt to elude the Coast Guard, the crew put up a dense smoke screen, hoping to vanish into the predawn darkness. At that point, Coast Guard captain W.A. Skeen fired two shots across the bow. When the *Geronimo* did not stop, a shot was fired at the wheelhouse, and the captain changed his mind. The tug was so heavily loaded that water came within six inches of its portholes. The five- to six-man crew was arrested and the Coast Guard inspected the ship, which had equipment aboard that allowed the cargo to be unloaded within an hour. Casey D. Ferguson, collector of customs at Detroit, said that this was the largest haul ever made by dry agents on the Great Lakes up to that time.

At Detroit, this federal prize tied up off Fort Wayne, an active U.S. Army facility, but while the case was pending in federal court, the *Geronimo* disappeared. When federal agents discovered it across the Detroit River at LaSalle, a suburb of Windsor, they were unable to recover it.

Then in mid-May 1930, the elusive tug reappeared as the *Amherstberg A-18*. Word was received by federal authorities in Chicago that the craft had left from Goderich, Ontario, on the southeast shore of Lake Huron; passed through the Straits of Mackinac; and was cruising in Lake Michigan. Authorities realized that it was the *Geronimo* repainted and renamed. It was seized off Green Bay with a cargo valued at $600,000 ($8.5 million in 2016 dollars). George S. Fitzgerald, assistant federal district attorney, started action to have the tug returned to Detroit.

FAITHFUL TO FISH AND BEER

Canadian liquor from Sault Ste. Marie passed on to Washington Island, Wisconsin, which was known as "Booze Island." In 1928, Everette "Butch" La Fond, a fisherman from Two Rivers, Wisconsin, went to the Soo with the fishing boat, *Faithful*. About to sail home, he was stopped by the Coast Guard and found to be loaded with a cargo of ale and beer destined for Milwaukee. Other ships from Chicago, Milwaukee and smaller towns sailed to the Soo for liquor while others met ships near Petoskey, Mackinac Island or Manitoulin Island, where booze was transferred to large vessels for the trip south.

COAST GUARD

Within weeks of the advent of Prohibition, violators were at work, and it is estimated by the Department of Commerce that, in 1924, two-thirds of the liquor entering the United States came from Canada. Sault Ste. Marie was in a strategic position for the Coast Guard to guard the border. The Coast Guard had the controversial and unenviable task of enforcing the unpopular Volstead Act through the Department of Treasury. In 1926, the American consul in the Canadian Soo noted, "To adequately guard the [St. Mary's] river it would be necessary to place Coast Guard men every few feet on the American shore of the river they [Canadian customs officials] say." The Coast Guard patrol boats played a game of hide and seek with the rumrunners and were naturally hampered by their inability to enter Canadian waters.

During the years of Prohibition, the Coast Guard maintained a varied collection of ships to enforce the law. The cutter *Tuscarora*, usually stationed at Chicago and Milwaukee, made trips to the Soo to show the presence of a large cutter, enforce the law and act as a recruiter for the Coast Guard. In November 1923, when it arrived for temporary duty at the Soo, it was commanded by H.R. Searles, who had been stationed at the Soo and was a familiar individual who could attract recruits. In 1929, the *Seminole* was transferred to the Great Lakes and aided in the rum patrol in the St. Mary's River.

The former World War I submarine chaser *Cook* was assigned to the western waters of Lake Superior to rescue local fishermen, help with recruitment

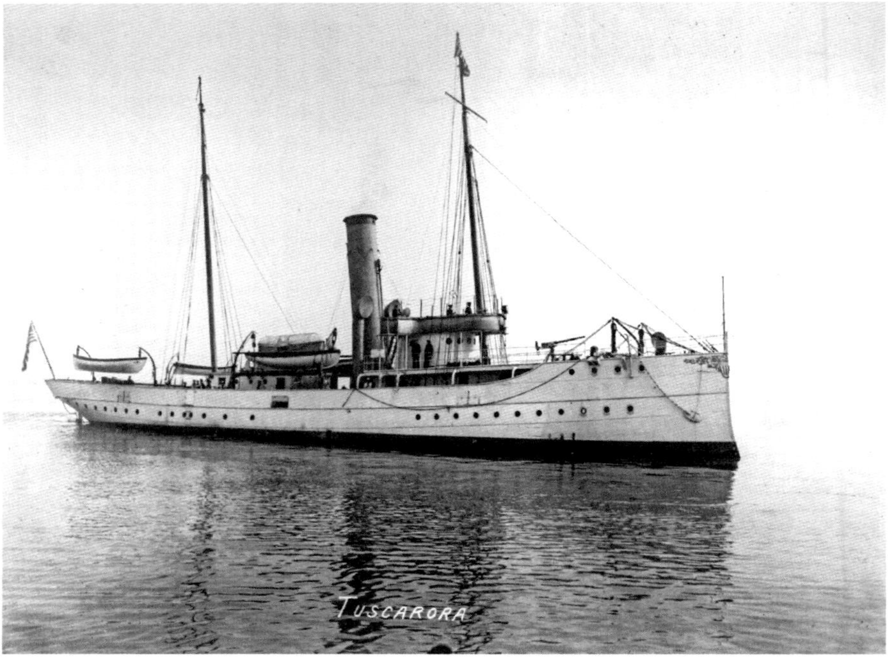

Tuscarora occasionally plied the waters of the St. Mary's River on rum patrol. *Courtesy of Still Picture Unit, National Archives.*

and patrol the waters to interdict rumrunners sailing south from Port Arthur. During the early 1920s, it was under the command of Benjamin Trudell with fifteen men and officers, and it had a cruising speed of eighteen miles per hour and forced speed of twenty miles per hour. In an interview with a Minnesota newspaper, Trudell indicated that he ran into few rumrunners while on patrol, although he did stop a rumrunner on its way to Isle Royale.

The 125-foot *Crawford* was launched in January 1927 and had been specifically designed to trail "mother-ships" that supported the smaller smuggling boats along the Atlantic coast. It was temporarily assigned to Sault Ste. Marie in March and then was permanently assigned to Two Harbors, Minnesota, in September. Newspaper accounts during Prohibition and later only report it saving lives and maintaining navigation; they do not indicate that it was successful intercepting rumrunners while on patrol. After a decade, the ship was assigned to Buffalo, New York.

Smaller Coast Guard vessels conducted rum patrols along the St. Mary's River at Sault Ste. Marie. The *Vigilant* (AB-17) was a harbor launch built in 1910 and was manned by two officers and four enlisted men and spent most of its carrier at Sault Ste. Marie. In 1933, it was stationed downriver from the Soo at West Neebish Island, a narrow spot in the river, to better intercept rumrunners. The crew had an arrangement with some rumrunners to protect them. At one point, the cutter picked up liquor and transported it to larger boats in Munuscong Lake and Mud Lake. The *Advance* (AB-1) was stationed at Sault Ste. Marie until 1924, when it exploded and sank. It was raised from the river, repaired and returned to service at Chicago. In October 1927, it returned to the Soo. There was also the twelve-ton *Sentinel* (AB-13) that was assigned to St. Mary's River patrol. The thirty-five-ton *Voyager* (AB-18) was classified as a wooden motorboat and was frequently stationed at the Sault as well. There were also a number of smaller vessels that patrolled the river from Detour to Whitefish Point, and given the fact that the river was filled with channels, coves and islands, this was a daunting task.

In general, the Coast Guard had a good reputation for enforcing the Volstead Act. In one study, on a scale of one to ten, it was rated a six—the highest rating for any federal agency. On the St. Mary's River and vicinity, there are stories of a lack of enforcement. Stories circulated that Coast Guardsmen would cross the river and visit the Canadian liquor warehouse on a social call and find out when a run of liquor would take place. Then they made sure that their patrol was operating in either direction but not in the path of the rumrunner. In 1920, when the rumrunner *Arbutus* landed at Eagle Harbor, some of the local Coast Guardsmen were involved in dispensing alcohol. In early June 1927, a consular staff member whose home was near Sugar Island submitted a startling report to the office. A Coast Guard vessel was anchored near Sugar Island and received cases of liquor from a rowboat from Canada. Over the summer, there were reports that two Coast Guardsmen were reportedly on a rowboat loaded with 114 cases of whiskey. There was little that the U.S. consul could do but complain to the State Department. Down at Mackinac Island, it was reported that a Coast Guard vessel had liquor on board and escorted other boats carrying liquor from Canada to the Grand Hotel.

There was also domestic rumrunning on Lakes Huron, Michigan and Superior. The ships engaged were commercial freighters and barges carrying lumber, coal and other bulk items. The liquor was hidden under the cargo and unloaded once the police had finished their inspection. Some of the many cruise and passenger ships that plied the waters carried unscrupulous individuals who landed at stops like Mackinac Island and sold tea-filled bottles as whiskey to unsuspecting customers.

SPEAKEASIES OR BLIND PIGS

The stories connected with bootlegging and blind pigs or speakeasies are folkloric, some of them legendary. With the onset of Prohibition, all 426 saloons active in the UP closed their doors. Suddenly, 12 soft drink shops expanded to 232 establishments. Some saloonkeepers got into soft drink parlors while others opened billiard parlors. Throughout the UP in 1917, there were 64 billiard parlors, and this number increased to 115 parlors. Obviously, there's no way to know how many of them were selling alcohol, but it's likely that many were.

In Calumet, several dozen speakeasies replaced many saloons, which had numbered three to five per block. Soft drink shops were on the first floor while the speakeasies were in the basement. In Shute's Bar, the patrons drank in the basement, and when the warning light went off, they went silent until the police moved on.

Edward A. Betts originally from Lower Michigan, settled in Marquette in the early 1920s and served on the city police force. Seeing the profits connected with bootlegging, he resigned from the force and opened a dry cleaners and press shop on West Baraga Avenue, within a block of the courthouse. By 1929, "Betts & Son" was known as Marquette's "leading clothes cleaners and pressers." To provide verisimilitude in his operation, he kept one of his children ironing clothes in the front window. All looked legit. However, he was obtaining liquor from a warehouse at the foot of Baraga Avenue on the Lake Superior shore where rumrunners docked and unloaded their wares. Then he brought the booze to his shop a few doors away. The buyer entered the shop with his coat draped over his arm and left it. Betts cut special pockets inside the coat and filled them with small bottles of liquor. The customer departed with his/her coat either worn or under the arm with no indication of the transaction.

One entrepreneur in Escanaba in 1930 held coffee royal parties in his home. The traffic and activity brought complaints from his neighbors and his family, who turned him in to the police. When the police raided the place, they found the odor of alcohol permeating the cups and room.

In Menominee, a blind pig operated in the same building that housed the police station while in Marquette, one was located across the street from the Federal Enforcement Office. Moonshine was delivered to passing customers in an alley near Iron River's city hall. At Harrisonville on Mackinac Island, partygoers filled their glasses directly from the dripping still.

Pricing

The price of liquor has to be gleaned from a variety of sources. Newspaper accounts from 1928 show that Chicago whiskey "almost always of the same make" but, carrying different labels, sold for $9.00 (about $124.00 today) a quart or $5.00 a pint, and gin was $4.00 a quart, "some in good looking bottles." In early August 1931, across the country a pint of moonshine cost $1.50 (about $21.00 in 2016).

4

Social Impact

Prohibition had a deep social impact on American society. It also exacerbated related issues and brought new problems to the forefront. Some of the issues involved women, youth, drugs, gambling, prostitution, dance halls and prisons.

Women

Women were directly influenced by Prohibition and the mores of the Roaring Twenties. Moonshining and bootlegging were not the domains of males only, as women quickly became involved in the manufacture, sale, transport and consumption of alcohol. At first, it was thought that women would not be arrested and convicted for liquor violations. In some instances, wives took the rap for their husbands and went to jail while the husband worked and provided for the family. The story of Lower Michiganer Etta Mae Miller—a mother of ten children who was given a life sentence after her fourth conviction, this one for allegedly passing a bag of liquor—was well known in the UP. An African American woman, Jennie Mitchell, from Marquette was arrested for possession but not convicted. Some women at Sault Ste. Marie enjoyed the thrill of smuggling liquor past customs officials in their clothing. Other women, such as Catherine Tomasi of Raymbaultown, acted as spotters and warning their husbands making moonshine when police were in the vicinity.

Widows found that Prohibition was an easy way to make more money than working in a dime store. Some widows operated stills in their homes and in the woods so that they would be disconnected from raids. One widow in the lumber town of Pequaming ran a still. Selling her wares at four dollars a quart, she was able to adequately provide for her family. Jolana Salani in Calumet operated an efficient moonshine bottling plant in her home. Women who ran boardinghouses made sure that their residences had plenty of wine or beer so that the boarders would spend an evening drinking wine at ten cents a glass, adding to the week's take. Widows operating groceries or laundries served drinks in a rear speakeasy to local customers or rented basement space to moonshiners. Some teenage girls were sent out by their fathers to deliver moonshine, figuring the police would not bother to stop them.

Given the liberation of the 1920s, women drank as freely as men. There were no restrictions on entering a speakeasy. One of the fashion accessories of the day was the highly decorated flapper bag, which usually matched the

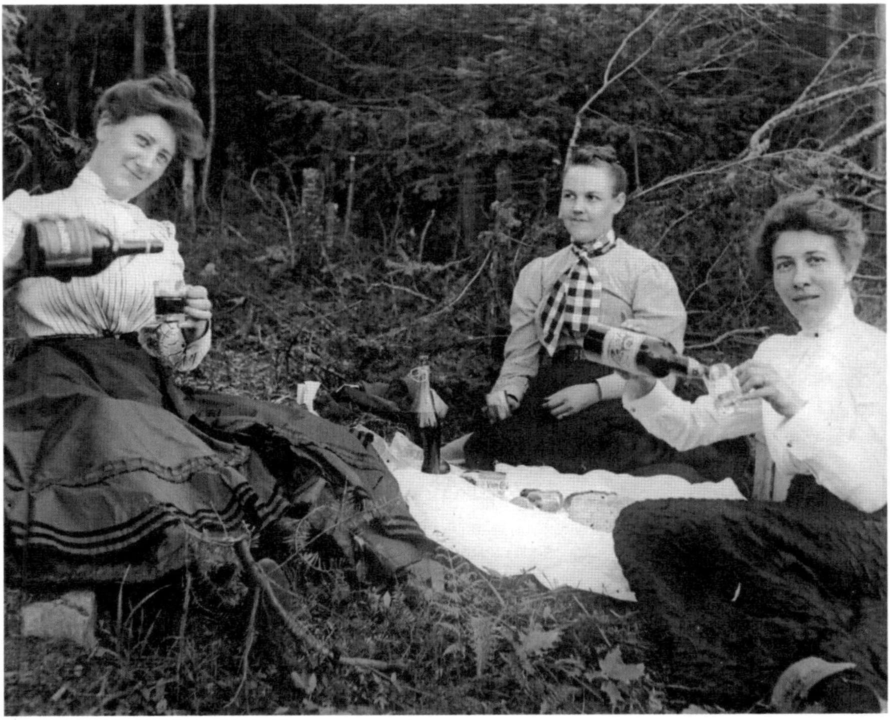

Prior to Prohibition, women were restricted from entering saloons, but speakeasies didn't require the same, an attitude that spilled over to daily life as women began to consume alcohol more openly. *Courtesy of Superior View.*

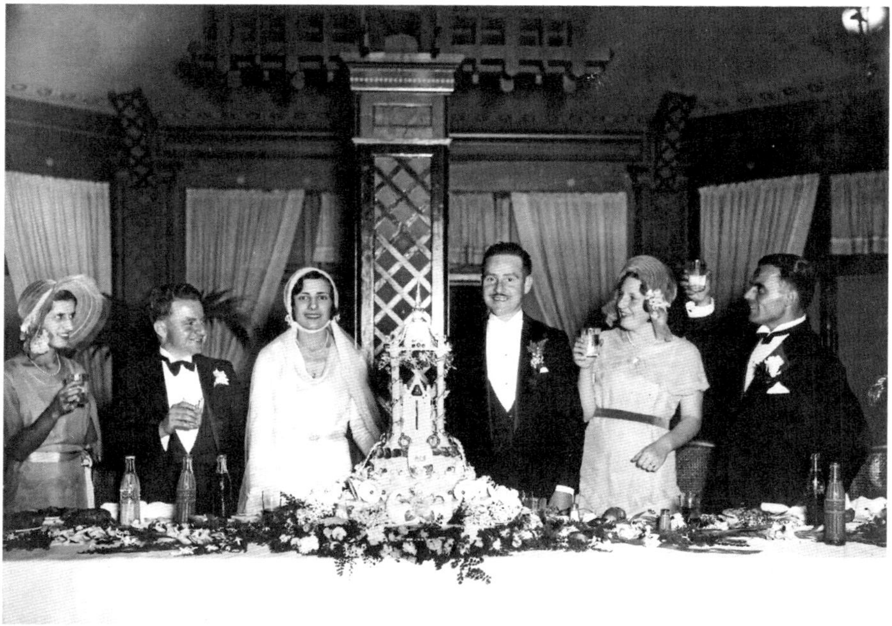

The wedding party toasts the bride and groom with glasses of orange Nehi soda, August 2, 1931. *Courtesy of R.M. Magnaghi.*

flapper dress. This accessory grew fashionable with the rise of the speakeasy and often carried a new necessity—makeup. The rebellion generated by Prohibition, late nights at the dance hall and the ready access to the automobile led to greater sexual freedom for many women, as well.

A diary by an anonymous twenty-year-old bride on her honeymoon provides a rare glimpse into two days of alcohol consumption. The first day started with a lime rickey enjoyed in the morning while a pint of moonshine was purchased in the afternoon to be followed by two glasses of wine and two coffee royals, and the day was finished off with a bottle of beer. The next day, the liquor menu included three glasses of beer, one pitcher of beer (shared), a gin fizz, a crème de menthe and a Scotch.

IMPACT ON YOUTH

Prohibition had a direct effect on the youth of the '20s since all state regulation of imbibing was nonexistent. Unscrupulous dealers readily provided liquor to youths.

As state prohibition unfolded, so did incidents of teenage drinking. A teenager from a prominent family in Marinette-Menominee was arrested for being drunk and disorderly. The police reported that they had considerable difficulty getting him to the city lockup since "he was simply wild from the effects of the whiskey given him." He said the source of the whiskey was Barbeau's Garage, so Henry Barbeau was arrested and charged with furnishing liquor. Ed Mantila of L'Anse remembered that teenage boys drove over thirty miles to Painesdale for a few beers to get "primed up" for a dance in Pelkie. In Calumet, a girl around twelve years of age and her younger brother donned large coats with specially cut pockets that were mobile liquor stores. Her father felt that the police would never investigate such small children. Throughout the UP, there were complaints of drunken teenagers having sex on the grass of nearby dance halls.

In reaction, the KKK bitterly complained about the breakdown of morals among the youth of the 1920s. In Escanaba, a group of Protestant churchwomen organized to bring morality to the dance halls and their

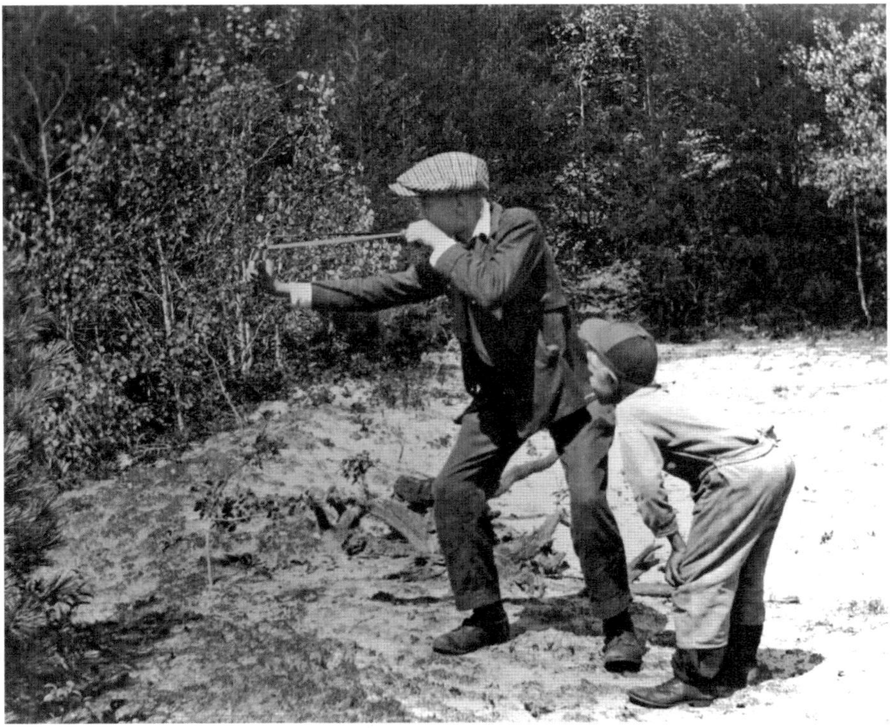

During the lawlessness of Prohibition, boys with slingshots were easily turned into auto thieves. *Courtesy of Superior View.*

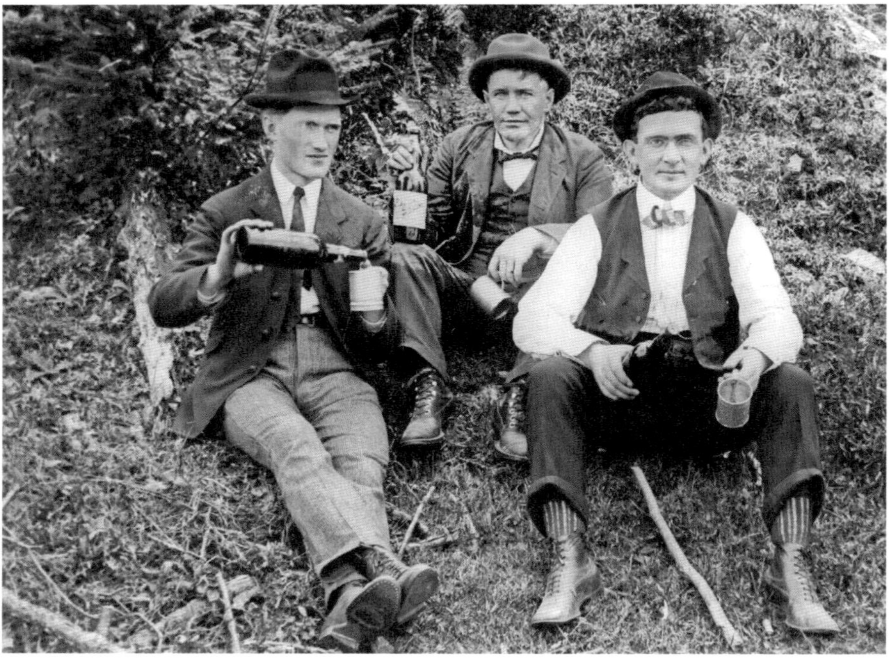

Drinking in the woods. *Courtesy of Superior View.*

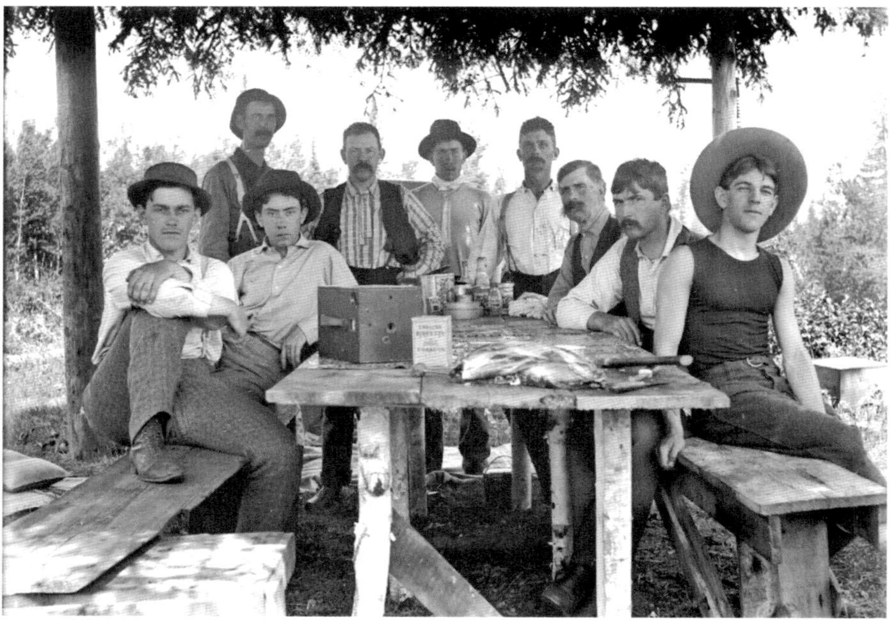

Young men and boys at a picnic waiting for the beer to arrive. *Courtesy of Superior View.*

children with the blessing of the Federal Prohibition Enforcement Agency and the local police.

Weiland's pool and dance hall in the small community of Trenary in the central UP became known as a hangout for teenagers where liquor was readily available. It was eventually raided and closed as a public menace. In July 1925, the Michigan Transit Company ended high schools' excursions from Traverse City to Mackinac Island because a few students, along with townspeople, had been "under the weather" because of drinking.

Teenagers were actively involved in the bootlegging business. In Escanaba, David Alperovitz was a teenage taxi driver who, between fares, delivered whiskey. Charles Bannon, born in 1920 and living in National Mine, sold old whiskey bottles back to moonshiners. Another teenager, George August, reported that "almost everyone" he knew was either bootlegging or drinking moonshine.

IMMIGRANTS

Protestant Americans and members of the Ku Klux Klan saw immigrants as un-American and pushed for restricted immigration that they saw as ruining the United States. When immigration was linked to Prohibition, their concern is easy to see. As James Rovano of Laurium noted, "You use water to wash not to drink," while Joe Meni observed, "If you were Italian you have moonshine" while everyone in Princeton had beer and wine without fail. For Tony Bausano of Calumet, "you didn't drink milk once your mother was done nursing you, because kids were given wine soon after." When Tony Jarvello of South Range had his soft drink parlor raided in February 1923, the police found a bottle of wine. He convinced the judge that being Italian, he was accustomed to having wine with his lunch and thus it was for personal use—not guilty.

Support for Prohibition and the American involvement in World War I received mixed reactions from different immigrant groups. Long supporters of temperance, the Augustana Evangelical Lutheran Church at a May 1918 conference in the UP voted to send a letter to President Wilson supporting the war effort and national Prohibition. Church members believed grain used in making whiskey and beer could be better used as food for the troops. On the opposite side, the Italian-American Federation of the Upper Peninsula met at the same time and supported the war but made no mention of supporting Prohibition. For Italians, wine was a birthright.

For Italian immigrants, Prohibition was the "dry time," but the production of wine and the grape skins distillate called grappa continued as before. Stills were made out of washtubs—the covers lined with wet dough to avoid a pressure build up and explosion—and copper piping. Once wine was made, the Italians would take the grape remains, add sugar and ferment them to a high alcoholic content and then distill it, producing grappa in the range of 150 proof. The potent drink was served with just a teaspoon added to coffee for a coffee royal, common among Italians.

The fraternal organizations tried to keep away from alcohol production. At the Duke of Abruzzi Club in Caspian, some wine was made, but the bulk was made by members at home and brought to club parties. This was also true of the Marconi Club in Princeton, where home-brew was commonly consumed.

Making moonshine was not limited to Italians. A Belgian immigrant, Theodore Meyskens arrived in Gladstone in 1921 and made wine only to be arrested for a minor infraction. His sponsor convinced the judge that he was a new immigrant who was unaware of Prohibition and got him off. Hungarians in the copper country made wine and plum brandy, as did Slovenians and Croatians, along with French Canadians. Other nationalities were engaged in winemaking and moonshining on a regular basis not so much because of their ethnic traditions as because it was a way of making money. Swedes in appropriately named Skandia were involved in moonshining as well. There were even "renegade" Cornishmen who turned aside their Methodist inclinations against drinking and followed the money.

The story of the Salani family in Hancock shows how they immersed themselves in a profitable liquor business. Alipio Salani was an Italian immigrant who mined in North Dakota before arriving in the copper country. During Prohibition, he opened a number of pool halls and speakeasies. Alipio developed a mechanism so that, if the police raided his blind pig, he pushed a button and the shelved bottles dropped into the sewer, thus eliminating any evidence. Raids were infrequent by local police, and the bootleggers were adequately warned when federal agents appeared in town. Alipio spent some of his profits paying bribes to avoid getting caught in raids. His wife, Folana, processed moonshine gathered by her teenage son, Babe, who drove the family Lincoln through the back alleys of Hancock and collected twenty-five-gallon barrels of moonshine and delivered them to his mother. Folana had a special ramp so the barrels easily rolled into the basement. There she opened the barrels of white moonshine, added Kitchen Bouquet to give it color and then poured the shine into pint and quart bottles.

Babe then took the bottles in gunnysacks and sold them to local restaurants and speakeasies. A pint sold for $0.50 ($6.81 today), and a quart went for $1.00 while a full gallon could be purchased for $4.00 ($34.64). The family home was an afternoon meeting place where the prosecuting attorney for Houghton County, reporters for the *Mining Gazette* and the *Marquette Mining Journal* and others dropped by for an afternoon cocktail or coffee royal. The family did a thriving business, and in his nineties, Babe said that they were never in need of anything during the Depression and even took a two-and-a-half-month trip to Italy in 1929.

Dance Halls

For parents and older generations, the dance hall was seen as the source of drunkenness and immorality. Youth could escape the restrictions of World War I through fast-paced and energetic dances like the Charleston, the Black Bottom, the Shimmy and the fox trot. The strains of jazz were enjoyed by the youth, but the more conservative adults felt that jazz was particularly decadent. Young people heard the music on the radio and phonograph records, watched the dances in the movies and were ready to dance once they hit the floor. The "flapper"—with her short, bobbed hairstyle; close-fitting hats; and short skirts—was joined by the "sheik," with his bell-bottomed pants. Casual was in, and the clothes were loose. They swayed, hopped and hugged, again to the dismay of the adults.

The music came from speakeasies, private clubs, dance halls and roadhouses. The UP was dotted with dance halls with such names as Terrace Gardens, Coliseum, Rainbow Terrace and Brookton, where they could dance to the Syncopators, Nightingale Orchestra, Le Duc's Orchestra, Arcadians, the Blue Melody Boys or Gunner's Jazz Band, where you could "hear the jazz bo's rip it up," or the Bohemian Orchestra with its "singers and entertainers." At this time, the ever-popular Viola Turpeinen on the accordion played with her orchestra around the peninsula to dance halls so packed that the crowds had to be rotated to keep the building from collapsing. The variety was unlimited.

There were two categories of dance halls. The first type were those operated by owners who were more interested in profits and cared little about social behavior. These establishments developed unsavory reputations. Alcohol was sold, which led to drunken bloody brawls and immoral behavior.

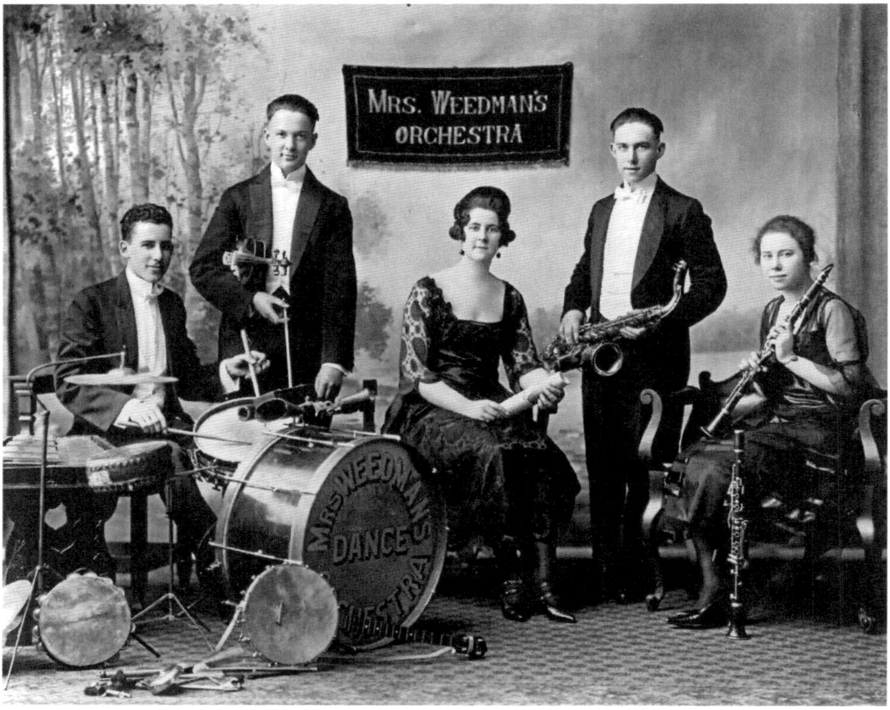

Mrs. Weedman's Orchestra (1930) was one of the many that played to packed dance halls throughout the UP. *Courtesy of Marquette Regional History Center.*

An example of "party without restrictions" was Orville Weiland's pool hall in Trenary, which operated as a dance hall in disreputable fashion in 1930. Young boys and girls were attracted to the place because it furnished them with liquor. The *Mining Journal* declared the place "a running sore and a breeding place of immorality and crime." It became known as one of the worst dance halls in the Upper Peninsula. Alger County authorities did nothing to close the dive, which was eventually raided by federal agents and Weiland sentenced to Leavenworth for two and a half years.

Federal agents and police traveled over one hundred miles to raid the Rainbow Dance Hall, which was selling liquor, in Menominee County. In June 1933, complaints continued in Iron County that the Whoopee Ranch operated without a license or permit and that it was a brothel dignified by the name "dance hall" that closed at 2:30 a.m.

The results were obvious. Drunkenness led to fights, lewd talk and behavior and auto accidents on the dark, narrow roads in the wee hours of the morning. The local and state police visited dance halls and sent in plainclothesmen to arrest gin swiggers. Police had to enter the fights, and many got beaten while others opened fire and wounded or killed assailants.

The Ku Klux Klan chapters in Iron Mountain and Iron River were especially upset and sent threatening letters to dance hall proprietors telling them to clean up the immoral behavior or they would be visited by the Klan, which would take the "proper action."

WARNING
TO DANCE HALL KEEPERS

Moral laxness at certain halls where "regular" dances are held has become so acute that measures must be taken to curb the revelry.

When girls and boys still in their teens are permitted to appear in drunken stupors and conduct themselves unbecoming young ladies and gentlemen, it is time that the best interests of society adopt means to correct conditions.

Notice is hereby served upon the keepers of such halls that they will be expected to enforce rules of respectable personal conduct.

Neglect to do so will bring them prominently before the public in an unfavorable light and their greed at the sacrifice of exuberant youth will be uncovered to public gaze.

Close observation of all public dances will be reported to this committee. Our advice is to elevate the standard of the dances. Please regard this fair warning.

Law Enforcement Committee of the
Knights of the Ku Klux Klan

[from the *Iron River Reporter*, circa 1925]

In Escanaba, the police met with a group of religious women from Protestant churches to enlist their support to end the reign of the dance hall. William B. Ormsbee, state representative from Flint who sought to pass legislation that would have forbidden aliens from having dances, raised the specter of immorality among the "aliens," or immigrants, and their dances. This was met with outrage by newspaper editors, who pointed out that the "alien dances" were better organized and monitored than those held by Americans.

The second category of dance halls consisted of those whose owners were concerned about offering the public good, wholesome entertainment and maintaining quality reputations. Liquor might be tolerated but order was kept. The number attending a dance depended on the size of the hall. The Brookton in Marquette could attract three hundred people. One of the largest dances in Marquette was the Intercollegiate Ball, which was by invitation only. One fellow was so caught up in the event that he went out and purchased a forty-dollar tuxedo for the dance, but he also wore it when he played with dance orchestras. There were also the New Year's Eve dances and a big dance on the Monday evening after Easter held in many communities.

The Terrace Gardens in Gladstone operated by Paul Wickert was one of the more famous and elaborate dance halls in the UP. It successfully operated throughout Prohibition and attracted the best of orchestras. In September 1927, Chas. L. Fisher's ten-piece orchestra, considered the best engaged in the area in years, arrived after a summer engagement at the Grand Hotel. After the Terrace Gardens burned in 1932, it was rebuilt on a grander scale and turned into a nightclub once Prohibition ended, attracting nightly floorshows from Chicago.

There were the invitational dances, sponsored by the Women's Civic League, Women's Relief Corps, Brotherhood of Railway Trainmen or even Northern Michigan State Normal School (now Northern Michigan University), whose dean of students Ethel Carey monitored the dates that women brought to the dances and forbade those she felt were troublemakers or bad influences.

Marquette Branch Prison

The Marquette Branch Prison was established in 1889 on the shores of Lake Superior. It came to be considered Michigan's "Alcatraz in the North" due to the difficulty not so much of escaping from the walled prison but of escapees' being able to find their way out of the northern wilderness.

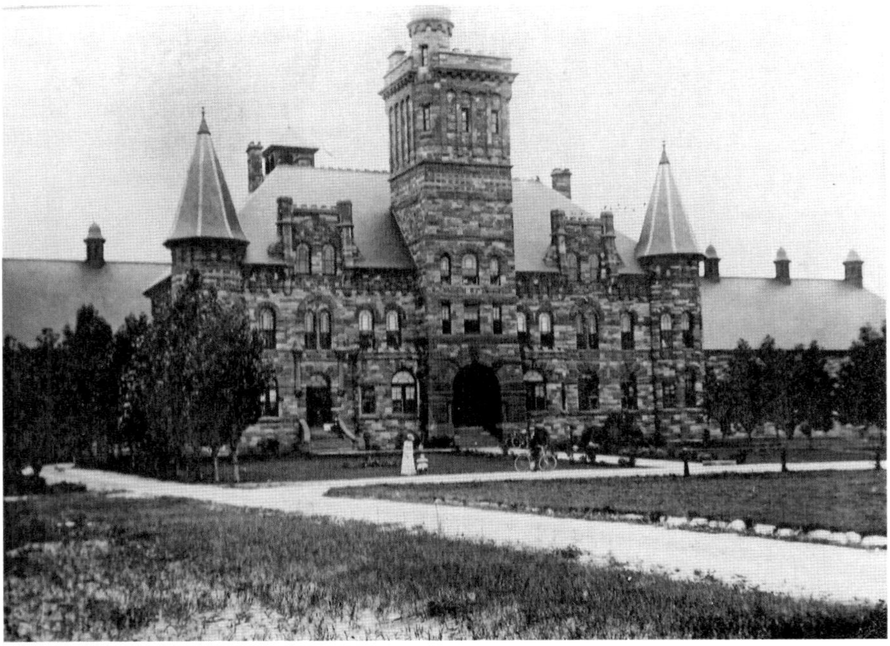

Marquette Branch Prison opened in 1889 and was home to many liquor violators. *Courtesy of Marquette Regional History Center.*

Although the prison had been built to house Upper Peninsula inmates, by 1920, 90 percent of its population came from Lower Michigan. Due to the violent crimes associated with Prohibition, the prison population increased substantially. The prison had cells for 666 inmates, but by the summer of 1927, there were 973 prisoners; by the end of the year, there were 1,022 despite several men having been paroled. Some 300 men were sleeping on cots in cellblock corridors.

With the rise in crime during Prohibition, a host of gangland convicts were sent north. Lax discipline and overcrowded conditions led to frequent murders of personnel and escapes. Arthur "Gypsy Bob" Harper attempted an escape in 1921, and he quickly tried again; before Harper's escape attempts, there hadn't been any in seventeen years. More escapes followed. In April 1923, Steve Madaja and Russell Smith escaped through the roof. Eddie "The Hand" Weisman, a notorious killer and "adventurer," and three pals went over the walls in June 1925 but were captured five days later. Weisman dreamed of more escapes from prison. Two years later, Leo "The Wolverine" Parent and two others escaped and were eventually caught in Duluth, Minnesota, after a series of bank robberies. The number of escapes from the Branch Prison were unique to the 1920s and have not been repeated in the present.

In November 1924, members of the Parmentye Shotgun Gang arrived in Marquette with a plan to help Weisman escape. They were going to attach guns to the bottom of a rail car, which would enter the prison. The Marquette police were alerted to the plan and summarily arrested them. In 1931, three members of the vicious and notorious Purple Gang from Detroit were convicted of slaying members of a rival rackets gang. The three—Raymond Bernstein, Irving Milberg and Harry Keywell—were given life sentences.

On two occasions, convicts killed prison personnel. On December 11, 1921, Gypsy Bob Harper and two other inmates in the prison theater attacked Warden Theodore Catlin, a deputy and his son and a trustee, all of whom died of complications connected with the knife attacks. The guilty men were frequently flogged, which was common at the time. Nearly a decade later, on August 27, 1931, three convicts entered the prison hospital and shot Dr. A.W. Hornbogen, whom they blamed for the death of their friend. The doctor and a trustee died, as did the three convicts, who all committed suicide. This era was the bloodiest in the history of the prison.

In June 1927, William J. McGrath, a journalist from the *Detroit Times*, received letters from inmates and family members about the inhumane conditions, widespread corruption and illegal activity in the Marquette

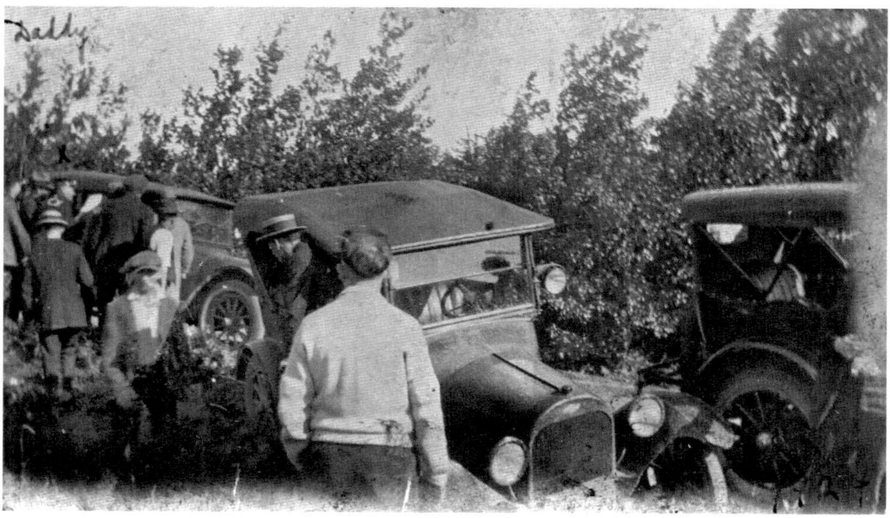

A Marquette prisoner commandeered an auto but was quickly intercepted by local police in Chocolay Township in this chaos of cars. *Courtesy of Superior View.*

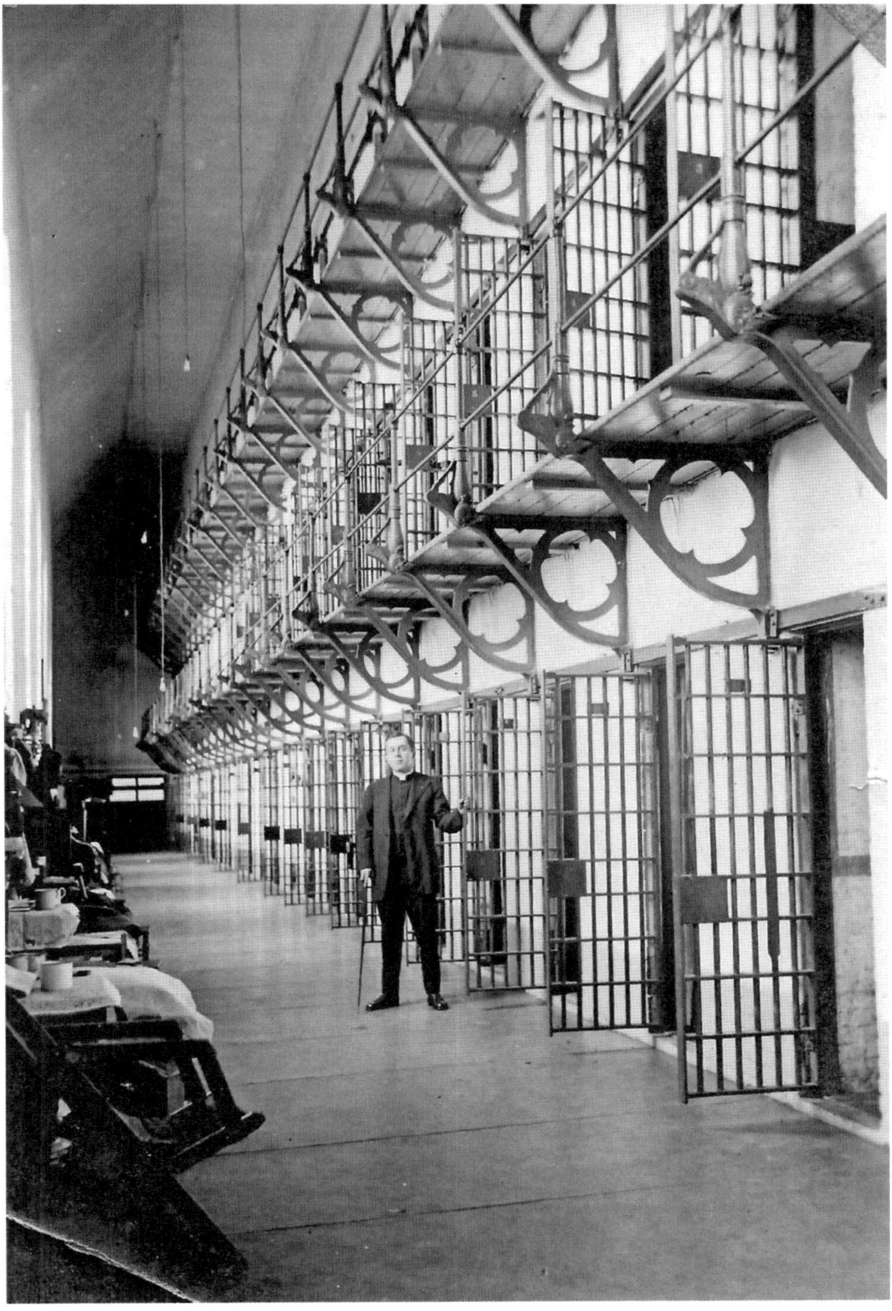

Marquette Branch Prison, interior. The prison saw its population greatly expand during the 1920s and 1930s. *Courtesy of Marquette Regional History Center.*

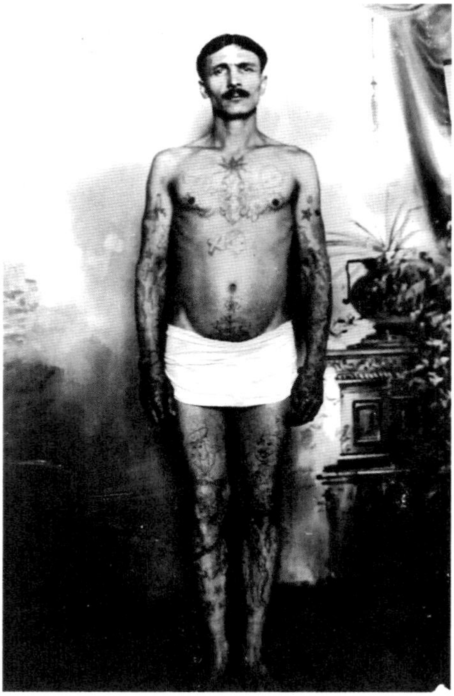

Left: Arthur "Gypsy Bob" Harper years after he and two additional inmates killed Warden T.B. Catlin and others in 1921 at the Marquette Branch Prison. *Courtesy of Marquette Regional History Center.*

Below: Calumet Brewing Company. *Courtesy of Superior View.*

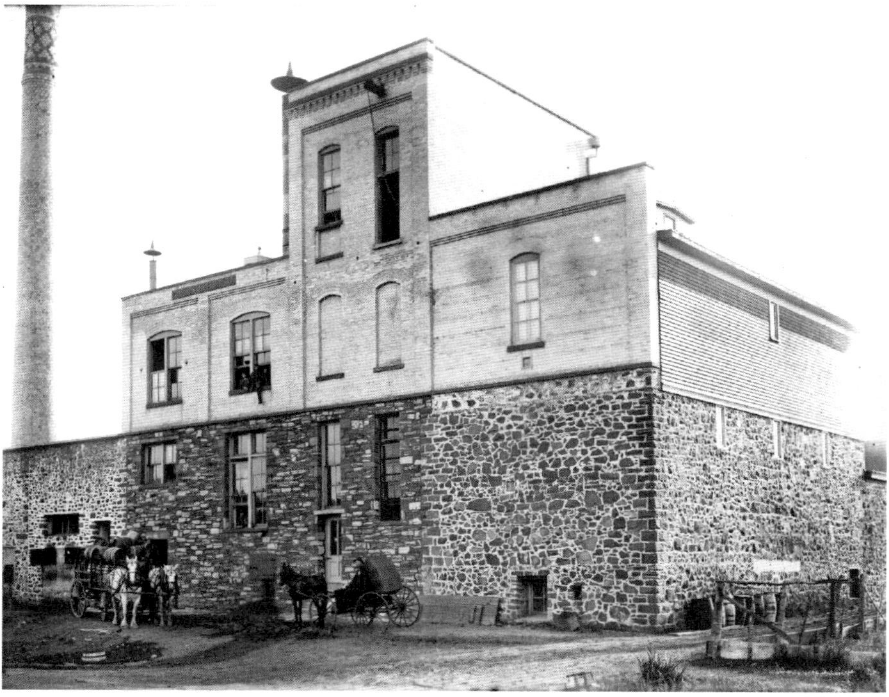

Branch Prison. He asked for Governor Fred Green's permission to enter the prison. Despite protest from Warden James Corgan, McGrath was allowed to conduct investigative reporting in the prison. Some editors, like those of the *Ishpeming Iron Ore* and the *Wakefield Advocate*, questioned the reliability of the "sob story" that was published. In his exposé series, McGrath pointed out that anything illegal, like drugs and liquor, could be had for a price. Morphine and other narcotics easily entered the prison and were purchased by addicts. Thanks to the connivance of certain guards, moonshine entered the prison and sold for three to five dollars a pint, and as one inmate informant reported, it was as plentiful "as water that flows through the pipes in the cell blocks." Prisoners without money to buy moonshine distilled their own liquor. They ran stills in their cells, in isolated sections of the prison yard and in buildings, using potato and apple peels for distillation.

The State Prison Commission met in late July in Marquette to investigate the charges made in the *Detroit Times* exposé. Even though its daylong investigation concluded that the exposé was inaccurate and Warden Corgan and his staff were given a clean record, it's likely that conditions were every bit as bad as reported. In 1931, the Wickersham Commission Report cited the Marquette Branch Prison for its inhumane punishments. And there were other convictions of employees stealing provisions from the prison warehouse. These are all another good examples of the corruption that was fostered by Prohibition.

The breakdown in law and its perception brought about by Prohibition was witnessed in many elements of society. In August 1929, when a number of conventions and the circus arrived in Ishpeming, a local entrepreneur went to work to make extra cash. He sold near beer to unsuspecting customers, who drank bottles and bottles of the stuff and were amazed that they could hold the alcohol, never suspecting that they were drinking nonalcoholic beer. In the meantime, the vendor made a $300 profit and awaited the arrival of the next convention.

Gambling

Gambling is another vice that has stayed constant throughout Michigan history, including throughout Prohibition. In February 1916, as state prohibition was being discussed, the chief of police in Negaunee, as happened in other communities, reiterated that neither slot machines nor any other games of chance would be tolerated in candy stores, saloons, pool halls or drugstores.

The Grand Hotel has a history of gambling and is rife with stories of the Prohibition era, many of them told by Bob Tagatz, hotel historian who provides visitors with a personal historical tour of the wonderful structure. As early as 1911, gambling on Mackinac Island was overlooked by state officials in Lansing in order to promote the tourist trade. Former governor Chase Osborn, writing in 1938, noted that twenty-five years earlier he had tried to enforce laws against gaming on the island and elsewhere but to little effect. Gaming on Mackinac attracted summer visitors from out of state, and the argument went that they were wealthy and were providing Michigan with money. Gambling centered on the large parlor at the Grand Hotel and was conducted after the manner of Monte Carlo, except on a smaller scale. It was so well entrenched that Osborn concluded that "nothing can stop gambling at Mackinac Island…except absolute prohibition carried into effect by an armed guard of either State Police or Military," but even then, he worried about bribe money. Osborn also exonerated himself and other governors who, he said, never took bribes but might have received campaign contributions.

With the coming of state prohibition in 1918, plans were made to attract affluent guests who would not have to worry about outdoor activities and recreation. The Grand was a mere sixty miles from the Canadian border, and there are myriad islands and waterways between the two. Guests were more interested in the best Canadian whiskey and real Scotch than questionable locally produced moonshine. The rumrunners were available to meet their needs from fast boats. The hotel was well supplied with the finest beverages. English Landing on the northwestern part of the island was an ideal landing spot: a road went from the landing to the hotel. Once the liquor was delivered close to the hotel, maids and nannies pushing it in prams brought it into the hotel. The management did not want to upset the Woman's Christian Temperance Union, dries or the authorities. In a less colorful manner, most of the liquor arrived through the kitchen door.

Once in the hotel, it was secretly housed within the labyrinth of corridors and over three hundred rooms. At times, bottles were hidden in spaces in the ceiling. Liquor was also hidden in fancy and elaborate radio cabinets. The hotel maintained a large speakeasy that is now the Brighton Pavilion, used as a banquet facility.

At one point, according to the stories, the Grand Hotel rented space for $15,000 a year, and professional gamblers took over a large suite and turned

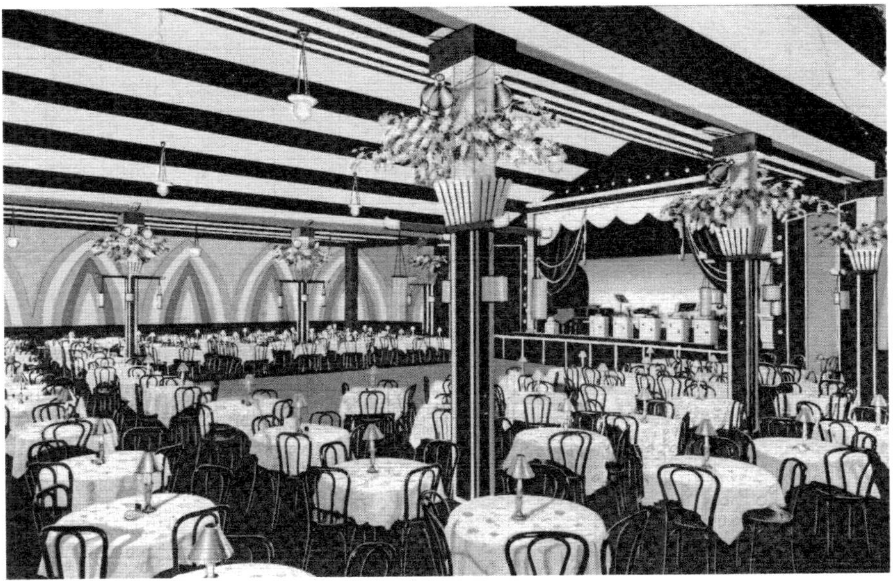

Dining room at the Grand Hotel, where fine food and beverages could be had. *Courtesy of Mackinac Island State Park.*

it into a gambling salon. The Egyptian Room became the casino, and a guard checked membership cards. Most of the gambling was done on the second floor, off the main staircase. These areas were outfitted with blackjack tables and roulette wheels, which could easily be "hidden" by collapsible walls. Liquor flowed, and few worried about being caught in a raid. A little old lady in the hall kept watch as she embroidered "GH" on towels.

In order to advertise the hotel and what it had to offer, management relied on a unique plan. It would have the local Mackinac County sheriff come over, raid the hotel and possibly find some liquor; then, the hotel would report the incident to the media. Soon, people in Michigan and throughout the Midwest learned that the Grand Hotel had liquor. After such raids, the number of guests rose.

Due to an exposé by the *Soo Evening News*, which sent a pre-publication notice to Michigan newspapers, the word was out, and the state police raided the gambling salon in early September 1919, seizing $30,000 (that's $410,836 in 2016 dollars) in gambling paraphernalia. Some locals were amused that this was an exposé, as gambling at the hotel was a well-known fact. A raid was made in 1920 that resulted in the seizure and burning of $20,000 in apparatus. On August 29, 1921, Captain Ina H. Marmon led a raid that netted $15,000 in gambling equipment, which included eight

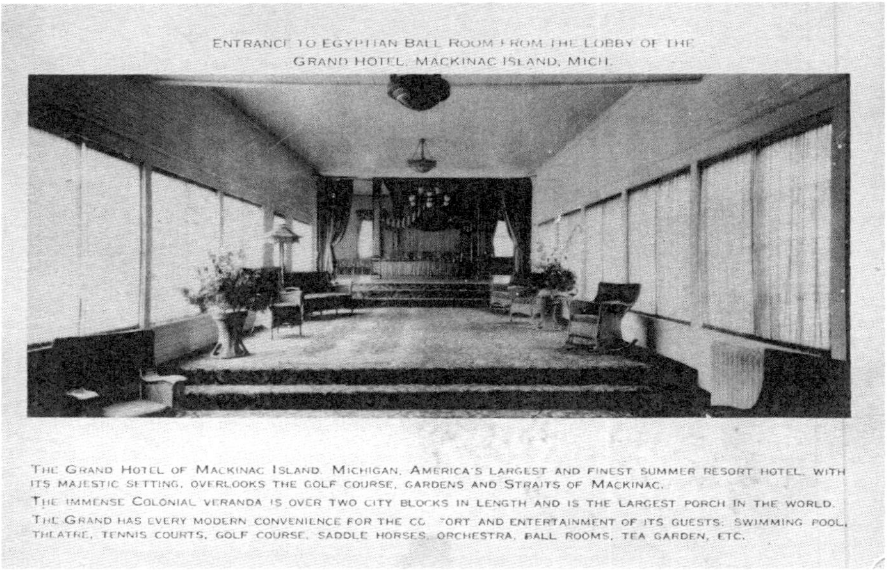

Entrance to the Egyptian Ball Room at the Grand Hotel, where gambling was popular. *Courtesy of Mackinac Island State Park.*

elaborate roulette wheels and tables made of beautifully inlaid wood mounted on ball bearings. The ivory chips had inlaid designs. Marmon reported that when the raid took place, the gambling was going full blast, with two hundred people playing, many of them women. These raids were in a sense a compromise by the state and the hotel, as they took place at the very end of the summer tourist season.

The Grand Hotel was thus able to weather the decline in guests by offering the public a safe and well-watered speakeasy where gambling was wide open. This also helped the hotel get through the darkest days of the Depression since Prohibition did not end and liquor was readily available until 1934, nearly five years after the stock market crash in 1929.

The Prohibition-era magazine *Plain Talk* provides a unique story. When the National Governors' Conference met on Mackinac Island in July 1927, a large part of the $25,000.00 (about $340,396.00 today) appropriated by the state legislature was used to purchase liquor. Commander Oscar G. Olander, head of the state police, according to the article, unwrapped the liquor bottles personally, handed them to Governor Green and encouraged the guests to drink publicly. Then there were some Michigan officials who turned over their "bar bills" to the state auditor to be paid with state funds. When an outside investigation was made, the detailed expense vouchers had disappeared. However, *Plain Talk* reported that Governor Green had personally paid $1,414.10 (or $19,254.00 in 2016 dollars) of the "bar bills." This type of activity undermined the Prohibition experiment in Michigan.

Elsewhere in the Upper Peninsula, gambling, which had been going on since native times, was commonly practiced on a small scale. During Prohibition, men would play cards, usually poker, in soft drink parlors and left the money on the table, not worried about being raided by the police, though many times they were. Illegal slot machines were around and periodically rounded up by the police, always reappearing later on. There were also punchboards, which the state considered gaming devices since candy and flashlights were offered as prizes.

PROSTITUTION

The coming of Prohibition enhanced prostitution with the rise of speakeasies and dance halls, as did the poor economic condition of the region during the 1920s. Liquor and sex provided money to people who were living on the edge of life.

In Calumet, there were a number of red-light districts. One of the well-known madams was Black Saddie, whose brothel was close to the railroad station. She and her girls greeted arriving miners, visitors and salesmen so everyone knew where the action was. At Sault Ste. Marie, home to several hundred soldiers at Fort Brady, brothels had existed for a long time in the area below the fort and the canal.

Marquette's court records provide specific views of prostitution. James Heade lived on the Indian reservation at L'Anse and came to Marquette to work at Northern State Normal School. He went to a restaurant–soft drink place at 111 East Baraga Avenue between Lake and Front Streets, owned by James and Irene Miller. The Millers' restaurant saw a lot of action, and a number of men played cards there regularly. On this occasion, Heade waited in the kitchen for female service, and he had nothing to drink but bitter lemon extract in his coffee. He was charged for services from the woman and then was told he could spend the night for fifty dollars.

Away from an urban setting, John Z (whose name I have changed to maintain anonymity) and his wife lived in a home in the farming country south of Marquette near Yalmer in 1923. He had turned his small home into a brothel and an outlet for moonshine. You could buy it by the drink

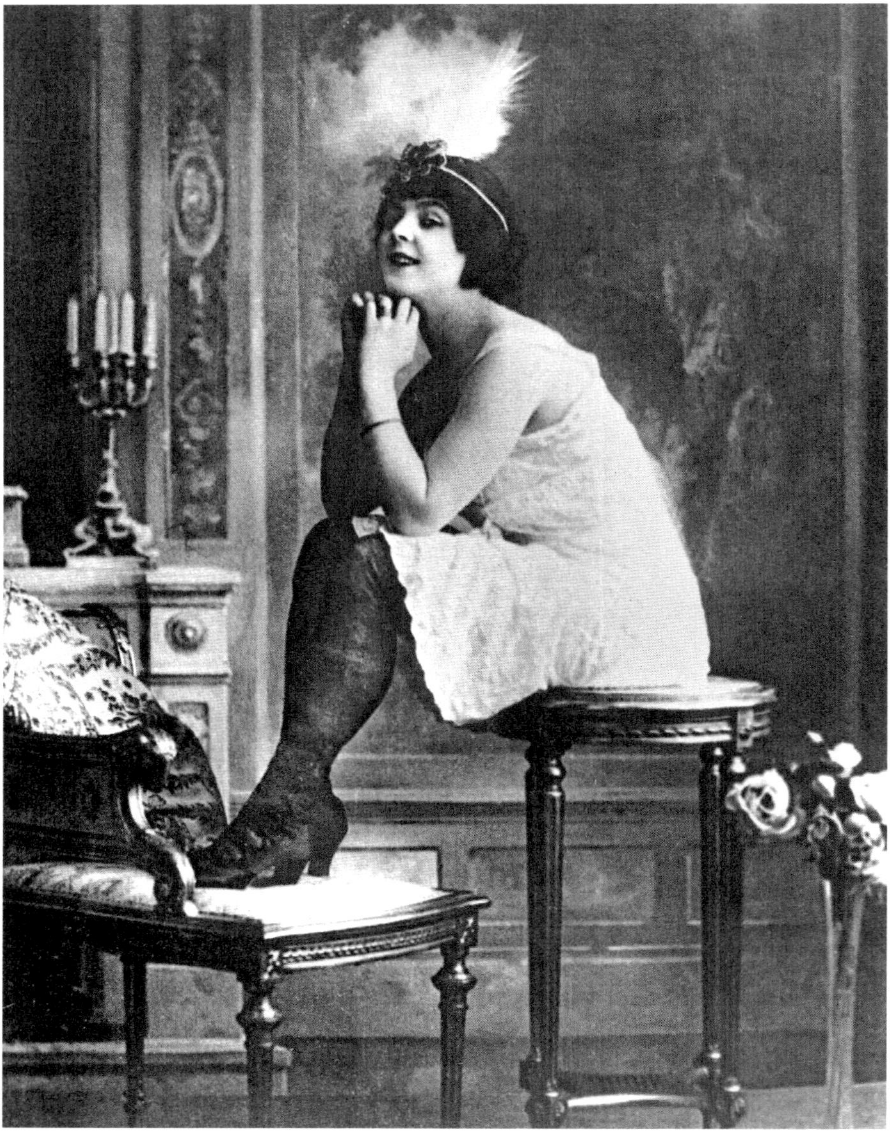

Prostitutes operated out of houses of ill fame or private homes. *Courtesy of Superior View.*

for twenty-five cents or for two dollars a pint and four dollars a quart. It was sold in beer or soda bottles. There was violin and piano music at the home. His wife operated the brothel out of a downstairs bedroom, and a curtain offered "privacy." The clients were Finnish lumberjacks from nearby camps and also men who had attended dances at a hall in Carlsend or Kiva.

"Entertainment" at times lasted until 3:00 a.m., even though there were four children in the small residence.

In Negaunee, William D. King operated the King's Inn in May 1918. A customer went to the hotel, registered under a false name and got a room for one dollar. In the process of going to his assigned room, he was given a slip directing him to rooms No. 4 or No. 24, where ladies were waiting for clients. The prostitutes charged two dollars, and they gave one dollar to King. The operation had been going on for two weeks when it was raided. Its reputation was known in the community. Beer was served in the room with the customer and the girl. There were also problems with the girls robbing their clients, with one Finnish fellow losing thirty dollars.

The Brookton Dance Hall, one of the more popular in Marquette, was known for a proprietor who provided the drink mix and ice cubes, but you had to provide the liquor—usually from a hip flask. Women hid the liquor in their purses, as no one searched them. The dance hall developed into a complex of structures. There was the proprietor's residence, a cottage where the big-time bands stayed and a little house next to the dance hall for the girls—a "pretty good business on the side." In general, many people felt that "dance hall" was a euphemism for brothel.

Drugs

Since 1873, the United States had witnessed the rise of addictive use of cocaine, heroin, morphine and opium. In 1913, Dr. L.F. Kebler, chief of the Division of Drugs at the Department of Agriculture, reported that 99 percent of all cocaine and morphine manufactured in the United States was used by persons who became addicted through medical prescriptions. A year later, national legislation, the Harrison Narcotics Act, was passed to regulate the production and distribution of opiates and coca products through the federal government, and this was followed by similar legislation in Michigan. However, by 1921, it was estimated that two million Americans were addicted, including physicians. This national problem played directly into the lawless era of Prohibition—the illicit drug market was more profitable than the liquor trade.

In 1920, a report from New York City classified the top most popular drugs available: heroin was the favorite, cocaine second and morphine a "bad third." The sources for illicit drugs lay in many enclaves fostered by the lawlessness of the era. Urban areas like Detroit and Chicago were supply centers, but morphine and cocaine were also found in raids in places like Prairie du Chien, Wisconsin, and fashionable resorts. In a July 1923 raid at Prairie du Chien, the police seized thirteen pounds of morphine and nearly four pounds of cocaine, worth $37,500 (about $519,552 today) to be used as regular adult doses. An envelope of cocaine was mailed to Hurley in 1922 and intercepted by the police, who established a connection with Chicago.

At the border, Sault Ste. Marie had been an important gateway for smuggling opium since the latter part of the nineteenth century. By 1908, drugs, especially cocaine, were available among the soldiers stationed at Fort Brady at the Soo. In a number of reports, the American consul at the Canadian Soo noted that drugs were finding their way into the United States through the Soo during the 1920s.

In the spring of 1928, a tragic situation took place at Sault Ste. Marie. Dr. Alfred A. Moody, a prominent Canadian Soo veterinarian, was arrested with a quantity of morphine tablets on his person at the ferry dock by U.S. customs. Detained, he committed suicide in the city jail. At about the same time, Sam Lee, a Chinese laundryman, and Albert Bensley, a local barber, were arrested at the Soo. Lee was found with $10,000 ($138,547 in 2016 dollars) worth of opium in his laundry, along with opium pipes, lamps, scales and other paraphernalia used by dope addicts. At the time of his arrest, Lee had on his person hypodermic needles for injecting cocaine and a quantity of morphine.

In 1927, several guards were bribed to allow drugs into the Marquette Branch Prison. A reporter from the *Detroit Times* during his investigation learned from inmates that if addicts had the money, they were supplied with drugs.

Although the law controlled physicians, some of them were known to prescribe morphine as freely as they would castor oil. It was not unheard of for people to steal prescription blanks and then forge a physician's signature to secure morphine. However, in small towns, such frequent use of a morphine prescription was reported to federal narcotics officers. In the fall of 1928, the police tracked two women who stole prescription blanks in Mackinac County to Sault Ste. Marie, where they tried to obtain drugs with a forged signature. They were arrested and tried in federal court. At other times, addicts broke into drugstores and stole morphine and cocaine before they were caught.

Addiction cut across social lines. Some felt that it was "nearly impossible" to get dope in small towns in the Upper Peninsula because of the familiarity of the druggist with his clients. However, in one small Michigan town a group of ten to twelve high school students tried cocaine on a dare. Then the doses became larger. One seventeen-year-old among the group became a "coke" fiend. A fourteen-year-old became addicted and kept his habit going by selling to twenty other students. An attorney in Michigan took heroin to get through a difficult trial and became an addict. In 1928, there were eighteen practicing physicians who were "narcotic slaves" themselves in the UP.

Steps were taken to alert the public to the widespread nature of the problem. In August 1928, Dr. Harvey A. Waite, state educational director and lecturer of the Narcotic Educational Association of Michigan, addressed the Ironwood Rotary Club on the evils of drugs as found in Michigan, the number-three state behind California and New York for drug use.

As *Mining Journal* reporter Manthel Howe wrote in 1929, "Just what a tangled mess the dope situation is, no one can realize until he has come in contact with it at first hand or has tried to help a victim take the cure." The use of drugs, though not as widespread as in urban centers, posed a social problem for residents of the peninsula and kept the federal narcotics agents busy.

Nationally and in the UP, the Masons, Knights of Columbus, Rotary, Elks, Moose, Eagles and Jewish organizations joined forces to alert the public to the drug menace and took action. Although Yoopers thought they were isolated, lecturers like Dr. Waite stressed that the drug traffic was big business and that when opiate addiction hit a community, it quickly spread through young and old.

KU KLUX KLAN & PROHIBITION

Due to the great social change that descended on the United States after World War I, the Ku Klux Klan arose to maintain the moral fiber of the nation—or the moral fiber as they saw it. The Ku Klux Klan was active in the Upper Peninsula beginning in the fall of 1923, when it was established in Manistique and then spread across the region. The Klan promoted Americanism, and in this case, it espoused the tenets of temperance. Prohibition became one of the Klan's leading issues. It strongly supported both Prohibition and its strict enforcement. The latter was a cornerstone of the KKK's "reform" agenda.

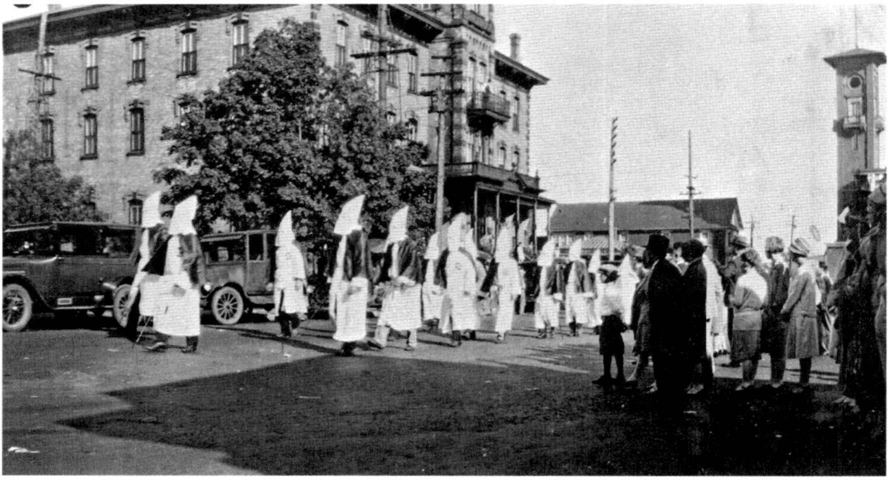

The Ku Klux Klan parading in Negaunee, Michigan, in 1926. *Courtesy of Superior View.*

The Klan was also virulently anti-Catholic, anti-alien and anti-immigration, concluding that Catholic foreigners were un-American. The Catholic Church had its own Catholic Total Abstinence Union, founded in 1879, and promoted abstinence through moral persuasion. The church did not want to get involved in the Prohibition movement, as many of its flock were European immigrants who used liquor responsibly as part of their culture. In 1916, Father F.X. Barth of Escanaba was asked to comment on all religious denominations promoting Prohibition as a political movement. He concluded that it was a serious blunder and un-American. Cardinal James Gibbons spoke out against Prohibition. He was "opposed to prohibition because it makes hypocrites of men." It is obvious that the Klan in the UP would tie this position to an un-American one and rail against the Catholic Church.

The Klan denounced the moonshiners, dance hall operators and teenaged drinkers and their carousing. In Iron River and Iron Mountain, it voiced its concerns about lax morality in the communities. In 1925, it issued warnings in the *Iron River Report* to dance hall owners who allowed teenagers to get into drunken stupors "and conduct themselves unbecoming young ladies and gentlemen." If the owners did not correct conditions, the Law Enforcement Committee of the Knights of the Ku Klux Klan planned to expose them "before the public in an unfavorable light and their greed." Members of the Klan also turned in bootleggers and moonshiners to the local police and, in some instances, accompanied police on raids. In Marquette, the Klan rented Aalto Hall, a former Finnish temperance headquarters, as its klavern.

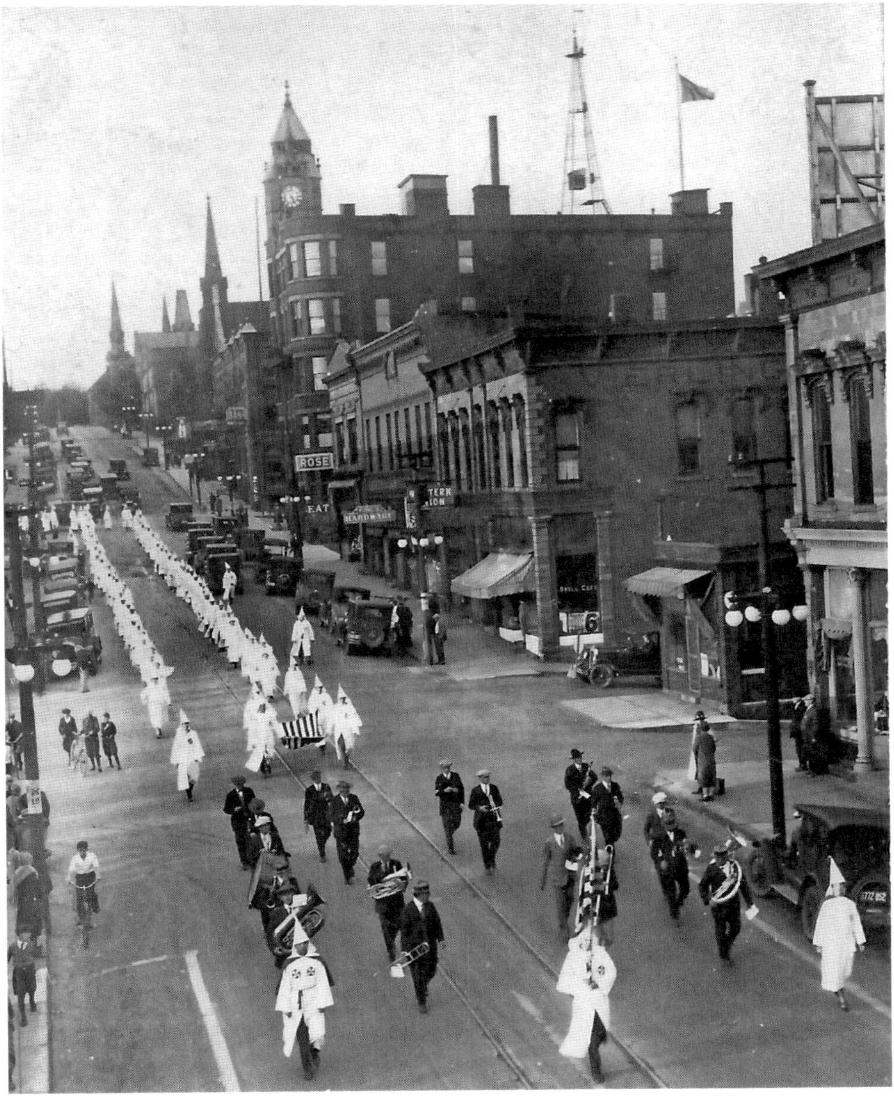

Ku Klux Klan marches down Front Street in Marquette, September 1926. *Courtesy of Marquette Regional History Center.*

What was the local response? George A. Osborn, editor and manager of the *Soo Evening News* in 1923, wrote that the Klan was encouraging patriotism, and since the United States is a free country, there could be no objection to the group and its goals. Most other editors took a very anti-Klan position and saw it as an un-American organization.

LITERATURE AND SONG

The topic of Prohibition worked its way into local literature and music.

The most famous was the writing of John Voelker, whose penname was Robert Traver. He is best known for his 1950s novel and movie script, *Anatomy of a Murder.* In 1951, he published a lesser-known collection of stories, *Danny and the Boys*, based on a group of woodsmen of the central Upper Peninsula. As Traver recounted, he derived the fictional characters by watching real people drinking in his father's saloon in Ishpeming. Danny, the central character, was brewing and distilling before, during and after Prohibition. As Traver notes, Danny "had his hands full distilling his moonshine and bottling his home-brew and shooting an occasional deer." Traver's style can be best seen in the following excerpt:

> *Danny had been making moonshine and beer at Hungry Hollow long before an obscure politician called Volstead had leapt to a dreary sort of fame by vainly dreaming that he could impose sobriety on a restless nation by legislative fiat. The only noticeable effect Prohibition had ever had on the Hollow was to place a greater strain on the resources of Danny's battered still, and perhaps to make Danny more careful. "They's more smellers and snoopers runnin' aroun' the woods these days than they's mosquitoes in our goddam swamp," he had indignantly snorted.*

The stories deal with Bessie the cow and the results of her eating buckets of wet mash, the results of a planned raid on Danny's still and liquor supply by the state police and similar larks. Then there is Big Annie, her brothel and the sundry clients and peculiar problems they faced. These stories work their way in and around Prohibition and provide the reader with a good indication of life during this time.

In June 1920, a budding author, Ernest Hemingway, published an article in the *Toronto Star* focusing on rumrunning "Canuck whiskey" into the United States. His world was a more contemporary account and highlighted activity on Lake Superior. Russell Gore, (1878–1954) a newspaperman with the *Detroit News*, was also a short story writer who published a number of stories focusing on the UP. One of these dealt with the heroism of the state police dealing with speakeasies and bootleggers.

Besides reading about bootleggers and stills in the UP, readers of local newspapers could find the exploits of violators around the country. There was a judge in a New York court who dropped the fine of an offender so he could find a job and provide for his family. In Knoxville, Tennessee, there was the fellow who had a three- to four-hundred-gallon whiskey well buried ten feet below his home in a residential section of town. Police became suspicious when a stream of people continually visited the home. He pumped whatever amount of whiskey customers wanted. Booze clubs popped up all over the country and catered to men stopping for a cocktail before heading home. Then there was Frank A. Vanderlip, a wealthy New York banker who bought up the town of Sparta and drove out bootleggers only to have them return to sell soft drinks and then quickly return to selling moonshine. There were the three New Haven men who fell into a cider vat—one was killed by being overcome by cider fumes. Boundless stories created a whole folklore found in UP newspapers.

Nationally syndicated popular poems appeared in UP newspapers that accurately portrayed Prohibition in American life. One in the *Soo Evening News* on July 23, 1923, sums up an aspect of the crisis associated with the era:

THE UNDERTAKERS' HARVEST
Frank Oster
July 1923

Drinking Extracts, Drinking Fluids,
Drinking Denatured real alcohol blue,
Drinking Varnish, Hair Tonic & Slime
Drinking mysterious concoctions combined.
Fusel Oil a Deadly Poison,
Found in moonshine booze,
Robs his victims of reason and sense.
No more earthly snooze.
Unknown Dopes not Used Before,
Hypodermics More and More
Morphine, Cocaine, Oh God forbid,
Let us of these monsters get rid,
God made poisons for a special use,
Not for weak humanity to abuse,
Each poison has a special mission.
Not to put mankind out of commission.

In October 1930, as the movement was under attack and seen as a failure, the following appeared:

WORRIES OF THE WETS
The time is coming, some sweet day,
Perhaps not very far away,
When people of this country may
Renig on Prohibition;
And when it comes, without a doubt
The folks who now must do without
Will find completely turned about
Over present day conditions.

Victor Records catered to ethnic audiences and issued thousands of records in the early twentieth century. In a unique musical development, Victor recorded a number of Finnish American Prohibition songs that sold well in the UP, home to thousands of Finnish immigrants. Elmer Lämpää (1894–1974) and Eddy Jääkkälä of the Minnesota Mesabi iron range sang "For Those That Love to Drink," recorded in Chicago in 1927. There were others in the same vein: Lämpää and H. Saarinen, singing "I'm Only Going to Drink" and "When I Was a Police Officer" and Tätu Pekkärinen and Mätti Jurvä, singing "My Old Wine Drinking Buddies."

5

End of Prohibition and Results

As the years of Prohibition passed, the public, even the dries, were disgusted with the results. It turned into a huge national conspiracy to circumvent the law. National Prohibition was a great mistake and not an ordinance of reason.

The rise in crime and total disregard of the Eighteenth Amendment and the enforcing Volstead Act led President Herbert Hoover to create the Wickersham Commission, which submitted its report in January 1931. It supported Prohibition but showed that the American public had contempt for it and that it was unenforceable on all levels. This led the American humorist and columnist for the *New York World* Franklin P. Adams to write a humorous summation of the commission's conclusion:

Prohibition is an awful flop. We like it.
It can't stop what it's meant to stop. We like it.
It's left a trail of graft and slime,
It's filled our land with vice and crime.
It don't prohibit worth a dime.
Nevertheless, we're for it.

The Depression had begun in 1929, and its harsh effects were being felt with the elimination of jobs and people unable to pay rising taxes. The Anti-Saloon League promoted the idea in 1916 that prohibition would totally eliminate prisons; instead, there was talk of adding new ones at taxpayers' expense. The governor of Michigan had to parole four hundred liquor violators to make room for future convicted violators. Stiff penalties, which were supposed to curb liquor violations, had not worked. Liquor violations and associated crime were out of control. An Association Against the Prohibition Amendment (AAPA) pamphlet claimed that between 1920 and 1931, $11 billion was lost in federal liquor tax revenues while $310 million was spent on enforcement.

Public reaction to Prohibition can be seen in the newspaper reports and editorials from throughout the Upper Peninsula. The editor of the *Marquette Mining Journal* called the Eighteenth Amendment an "unenforceable law." In March 1930, the *Ironwood Times* editor C.E. Bennett summed up the effects of Prohibition on the UP and the nation: "Crime, drinking to excess by school children, homes turned into saloons, poison liquor, a greater contempt for all laws than ever in history—chiefly because the nation has learned contempt for one law and the upcoming generation is not disposed to differentiate." A reporter for the same paper in October 1933 wrote that the record of enforcement of Prohibition in the UP and the Western District of Michigan was a "waste and futility of experiment in control of habit by law." Hundreds were convicted, the prisons were filled and all of this was a tremendous burden to the public treasury. A December 1933 newspaper article concluded that Prohibition was the "most vicious legal enactment ever attempted in this country" and that it "resulted in a tremendous increase in the drinking of liquor by women, even girls and boys, brought to the front the bootlegger who sold a terrible quality of booze at high prices and used much of the large sums of money realized from the illegal traffic for the protection of criminals."

Throughout the nation and Michigan, various organizations were established or activated to end Prohibition. The Crusaders, Michigan Moderation League, the Women's Organization for National Prohibition Reform and the Association Against the Prohibition Amendment organized and finally broke the back of the Anti-Saloon League.

Across the United States, congressmen who had been bullied to support Prohibition by the Anti-Saloon League turned to reason. In the UP, Representative Frank P. Bohn of Newberry in February 1931 announced that, although he had supported prohibition in 1916, his support was ended. For him, the bootlegger, hijacker and speakeasy had replaced the saloon and its evils. More and more, thinking people in Michigan were going in this direction.

By the early 1930s, anti-Prohibition women's groups had formed and gathered momentum. During the 1932 presidential campaign, Franklin

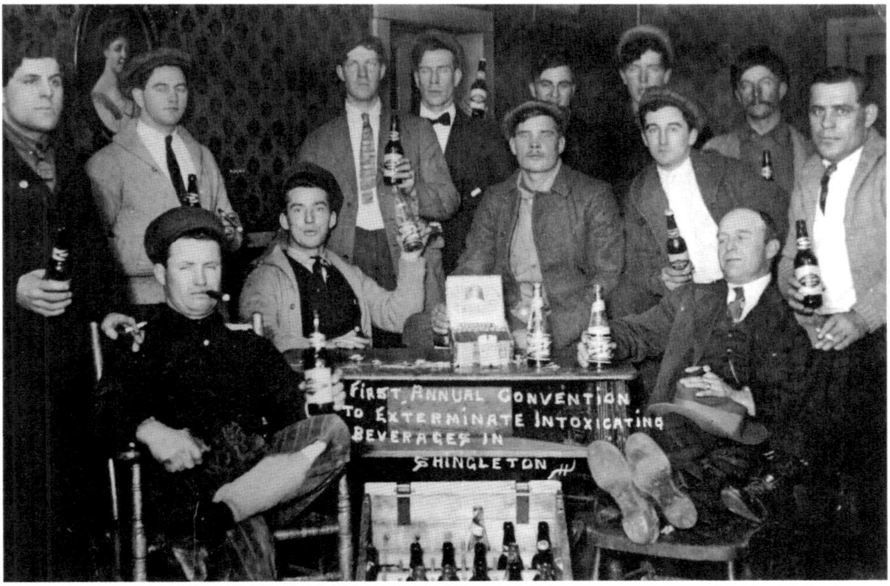

"First Annual Convention to Exterminate Intoxicating Beverages" held in Shingleton, Michigan. *Courtesy of Superior View.*

D. Roosevelt called for the end of Prohibition. Besides all of its faults, Prohibition allowed liquor to be freely made and sold without any revenue being collected while millions of dollars were spent enforcing the law.

The people of Michigan responded and in 1932 overwhelmingly approved the repeal of the state prohibition amendment. On April 10, 1933, Michigan was the first state to ratify the Twenty-First Amendment, and by December 5 (Repeal Day), national Prohibition was over. Michigan elected to become a "monopoly state," where the state government set up the control of the liquor business through the Liquor Control Commission (LCC). The production, distribution and sale of beer, spirits and wine would be handled by separate private entities. Saloons, which had existed in the hundreds prior to Prohibition, were now under tighter control by the LCC and fewer in number. Communities in the UP that prior to Prohibition had forty to fifty saloons after its repeal might have a dozen or so—a long-term effect of Prohibition.

With repeal, few of the UP breweries reopened. In Escanaba, the Richter Brewery reopened as Delta Brewing. The Soo Brewery also reopened, but both of them lasted only a few years. Haas and Bosch Brewing in the copper country became the dominant breweries in the UP, but Haas fell victim to changing markets and was the next one to close. Bosch did its best to remain

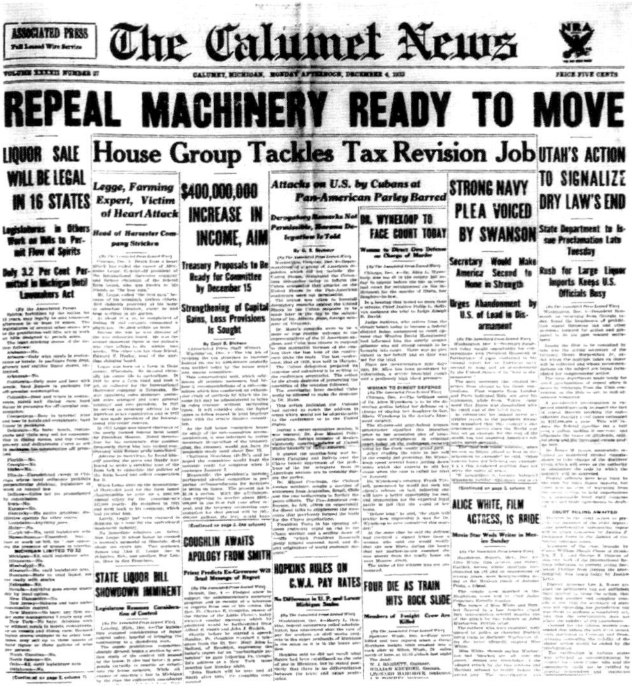

ASSOCIATED PRESS

The Calumet News

REPEAL MACHINERY READY TO MOVE

LIQUOR SALE WILL BE LEGAL IN 16 STATES

House Group Tackles Tax Revision Job

Legge, Farming Expert, Victim of Heart Attack

$400,000,000 INCREASE IN INCOME, AIM

Treasury Proposals to Be Ready for Committee by December 15

Attacks on U.S. by Cubans at Pan-American Parley Barred

DR. WYNEKOOP TO FACE COURT TODAY

STRONG NAVY PLEA VOICED BY SWANSON

Secretary Would Make America Second to None in Strength

UTAH'S ACTION TO SIGNALIZE DRY LAW'S END

COUGHLIN AWAITS APOLOGY FROM SMITH

STATE LIQUOR BILL SHOWDOWN IMMINENT

HOPKINS RULES ON C.W.A. PAY RATES

FOUR DIE AS TRAIN HITS ROCK SLIDE

ALICE WHITE, FILM ACTRESS, IS BRIDE

Left: *Calumet News* (1933). *Courtesy of 906 Heritage, James Shefchik.*

Below: With the end of Prohibition in December 1933, liquor stores around the United States were stocked for business. *Courtesy of Still Picture Unit National Archives.*

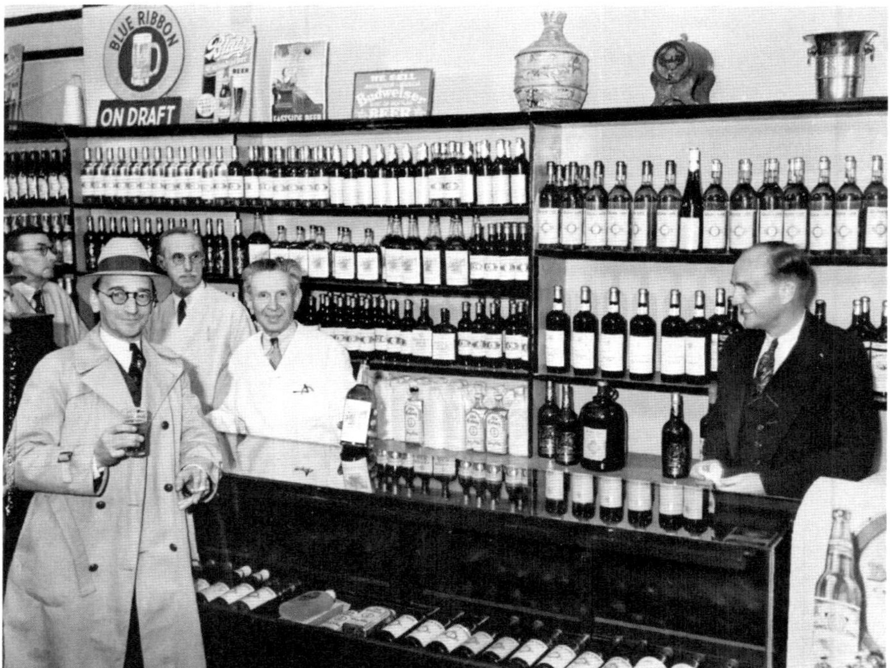

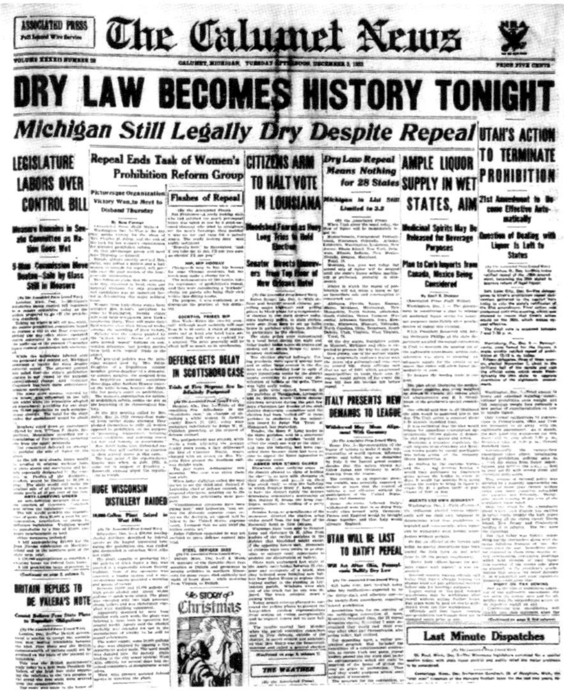

ASSOCIATED PRESS Full Leased Wire Service

The Calumet News

DRY LAW BECOMES HISTORY TONIGHT

Michigan Still Legally Dry Despite Repeal

UTAH'S ACTION TO TERMINATE PROHIBITION

21st Amendment to Become Effective Automatically

LEGISLATURE LABORS OVER CONTROL BILL

Repeal Ends Task of Women's Prohibition Reform Group

Flashes of Repeal

CITIZENS ARM TO HALT VOTE IN LOUISIANA

Dry Law Repeal Means Nothing for 28 States

AMPLE LIQUOR SUPPLY IN WET STATES, AIM

Medicinal Spirits May Be Released for Beverage Purposes

Plan to Curb Imports from Canada, Mexico Being Considered

DEFENSE GETS DELAY IN SCOTTSBORO CASE

ITALY PRESENTS NEW DEMANDS TO LEAGUE

HUGE WISCONSIN DISTILLERY RAIDED

UTAH WILL BE LAST TO RATIFY REPEAL

BRITAIN REPLIES TO DE VALERA'S NOTE

The Story of Christmas

Last Minute Dispatches

Left: *Calumet News* (1933). *Courtesy of 906 Heritage, James Shefchik.*

Below: With the end of Prohibition, saloons were ready to serve once again. *Courtesy of Superior View.*

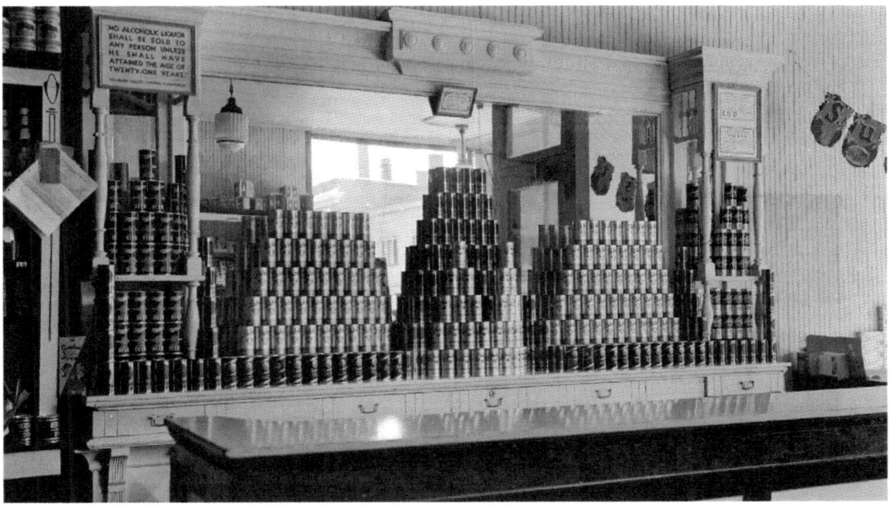

in business by modernizing equipment and space and bringing forth new products like Sauna beer, but it, too, had to close in late 1973. As with other regional breweries, the UP breweries, although they had a fine product, they did not have the advertising budget to compete with the giant national breweries like Miller, Budweiser or Pabst. The UP did not see a revival in

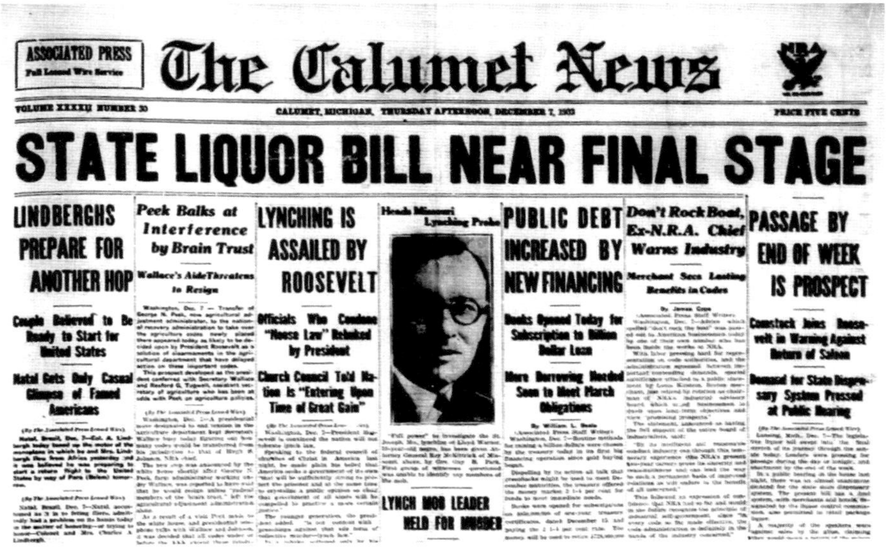

ASSOCIATED PRESS
Full Leased Wire Service

The Calumet News

CALUMET, MICHIGAN, THURSDAY AFTERNOON, DECEMBER 7, 1933

PRICE FIVE CENTS

STATE LIQUOR BILL NEAR FINAL STAGE

LINDBERGHS PREPARE FOR ANOTHER HOP

Couple Believed to Be Ready to Start for United States

Natal Gets Only Casual Glimpse of Famed Americans

Peek Balks at Interference by Brain Trust

Wallace's Aide Threatens to Resign

LYNCHING IS ASSAILED BY ROOSEVELT

Officials Who Condone "Noose Law" Rebuked by President

Church Council Told Nation Is "Entering Upon Time of Great Gain"

LYNCH MOB LEADER HELD FOR MURDER

PUBLIC DEBT INCREASED BY NEW FINANCING

Books Opened Today for Subscription to Billion Dollar Loan

More Borrowing Needed Soon to Meet March Obligations

Don't Rock Boat, Ex-N.R.A. Chief Warns Industry

Merchant Sees Lasting Benefits in Codes

PASSAGE BY END OF WEEK IS PROSPECT

Comstock Joins Roosevelt in Warning Against Return of Saloon

Demand for State Dispensary System Pressed at Public Hearing

Calumet News (1933). *Courtesy of 906 Heritage, James Shefchik.*

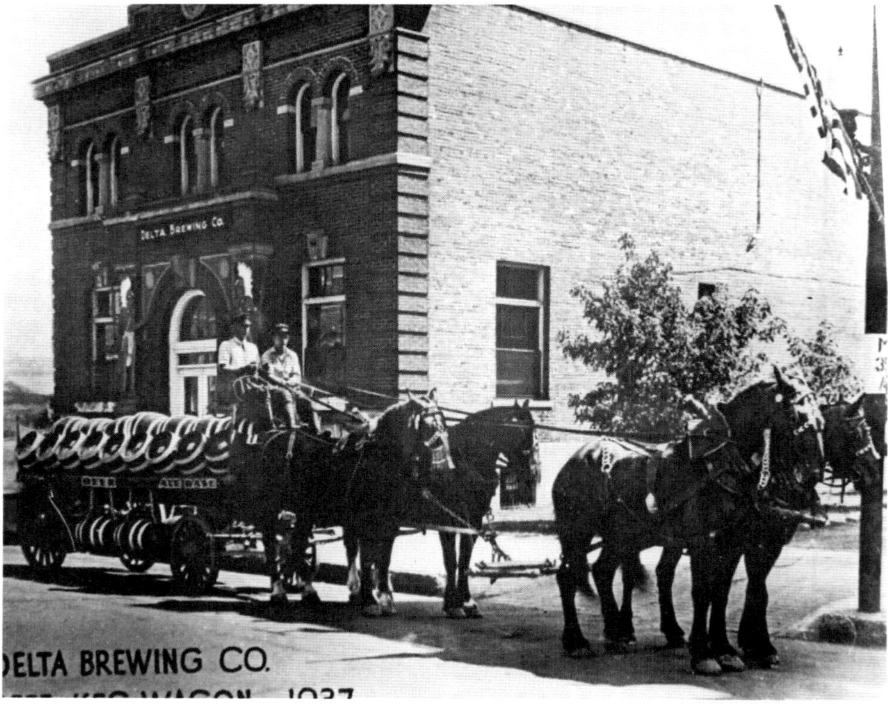

Delta Beverage Company reopened and in 1937 re-created the olden days with this beer keg wagon. (Escanaba). *Courtesy of Superior View.*

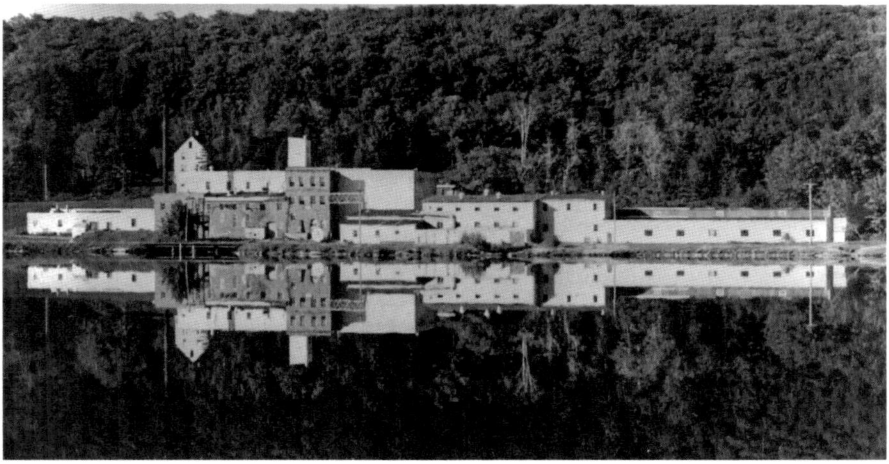

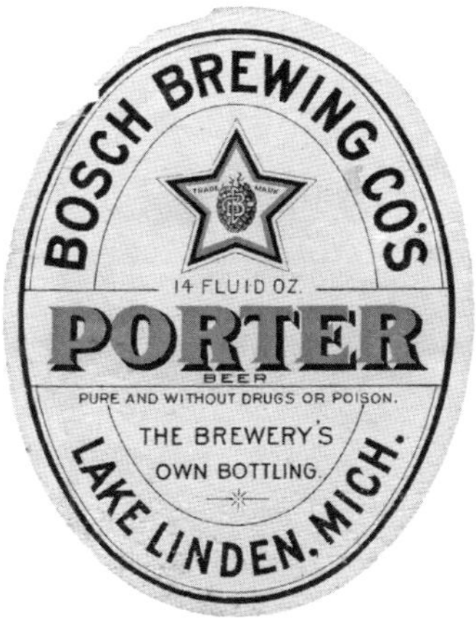

Top: Bosch Brewery. *Courtesy of Superior View.*

Above: Bosch Porter Beer label. *Courtesy of Brian Stechschulte*

brewing until Escanaba's Hereford & Hops Brew Pub opened in 1994. Today, there are more breweries—seventeen—operating in the UP than existed in pre-Prohibition days.

The repeal of the Eighteenth Amendment was welcomed by people throughout the Upper Peninsula. For many, their lives would no longer focus on liquor. However, as the State of Michigan implemented new licensing and delivery policies through the Liquor Control Commission, moonshining continued on a declining basis. It had become a big business, and stills were operating in the woods; however, now there were alternatives—quality liquor was available, and taverns and liquor stores licensed by the state opened. There was no need for these illicit outlets, but a number of them lasted throughout the decade of the 1930s in many parts of the UP.

The rise and fall of Prohibition, both nationally and locally in the UP, showed the folly of trying to alter human behavior through legislation. The results were far worse and destructive than the vices brought about by the old-time saloon.

6
Touring Prohibition Sites

Across the Upper Peninsula and on the Wisconsin line, there are a variety of sites and taverns that trace their origins to Prohibition days. Pre-Prohibition brewery art survived in the copper country. At the Ambassador Bar and Grill in Houghton, the Bosch brewery created whimsical elves involved with beer making that covered the walls of the original saloon. Fortunately, the owners, possibly having a premonition that Prohibition would eventually end, rolled up the canvas paintings and stored them in the basement. They were replaced after Prohibition. The same is true of the Michigan Café, home to the Calumet Brewing Company. Here scenes of German peasants enjoying beer cover the ceiling of the bar. These examples of art rescued from destruction during Prohibition are available to patrons of these establishments.

Up the street from the Michigan Café in Calumet is Shute's on Sixth Street with a decorated bar dating from the 1890s. During Prohibition, the speakeasy was located in the basement.

With the end of Prohibition, three Italian Americans—Tony Gagliardi, Louis Bonetti and Jim Nardi—opened some of the earliest taverns in Ishpeming in 1934. They were so pleased with the end of the era that they honored those who helped end Prohibition by naming their bars the Roosevelt, the Senate and the Congress. The last of these is still in operation and is known for its pizza and its convivial, community-oriented atmosphere.

Cognition Brewpub in Ishpeming is located in the former Mather Inn (now condos), which opened in 1932. Originally, the area was a staff-changing area, but with the end of Prohibition, it reopened as the Tap Room and remains today.

The Antlers Bar/Restaurant in Sault Ste. Marie was originally called the Bucket of Blood and Ice Cream Parlor. During Prohibition, it was an ice cream parlor that sold a gallon of ice cream a month though it showed a profit of $900. It is known for its legends, ghost stories, the basement speakeasy and walls and a ceiling now filled with stuffed animals.

Ed and Violet Horn opened Horn's Bar and Restaurant on Mackinac Island during Prohibition. They operated a pool hall and snack shop on the first floor and a speakeasy that catered to members of the notorious Purple Gang when they visited Mackinac Island. It is reputed to be the first tavern or one of the first in Michigan to be licensed in 1933. It remains one of the island's nightspots during the summer.

At the Grand Hotel, of course, liquor flowed, and gambling kept patrons busy. The Brighton Pavilion in the hotel was the original site for the speakeasy during Prohibition and is on the hotel tour. A few miles to the east in Hessel on the mainland is the E.J. Mertaugth Boat Works, the first Chris Craft distributor (1925) that is still operating. Annually, on the second Saturday in August, a classic wooden boat festival includes former rumrunners such as Ned Fenlon's *Quiet Please.*

Just across the border in Wisconsin are two Prohibition-related sites. One is the town of Hurley with its bars and designation as the "strip club capital of the U.S." Washington Island is just outside the watery border of the UP. Since angostura bitters were consumed in both locations, Nelsen's Bitter Hall is included on the tour. A Danish immigrant, Tom Nelsen opened the tavern in 1899. When Prohibition began, he refused to close and applied for and received a pharmacist license to dispense bitters as a "stomach tonic for medicinal purposes." He served angostura bitters with 90 percent alcohol. It is the oldest legal continually operated tavern in Wisconsin and nearby Upper Peninsula. Drink a shot and receive a Bitter's Club Certificate. It also sells the most angostura in the world.

7
Cocktails on the Border

The Upper Peninsula was a rough-and-tumble environment, with few fancy nightclubs during Prohibition. However, there were pockets of upscale resorts where affluent midwesterners spent their summers. One of these was the Grand Hotel, where fine food, imported liquor from Canada and cocktails were available. Elsewhere in the UP, the liquor was listed as "good" and "not-so-good" and was readily available at speakeasies like "Poker Joe," Horn's Place, "Shorty" Perron's Restaurant or Leo Shepky's Place. You could also buy it in nightclubs like the Terrace Gardens and the Brookton. A secret language developed for ordering drinks, especially at soda shops. The patron would tell the bartender, "Give me a ginger ale" and then waited for the bartender to wink and knowingly reply, "Imported or domestic?" To the answer "imported," he served the patron a highball.

The following are some of the little-known drinks that were popular in the Upper Peninsula during Prohibition.

Anaconda

The Beach Inn was a popular resort hotel on the shore of Munising Bay in the first half of the twentieth century. It became famous for its Anaconda, which lasted through Prohibition and into the 1950s, when the Beach Inn closed. It is probably the most iconic cocktail from the UP. Any liquor can be used, but the white liquors allow the maple flavor to stand out.

1 to 2 ounces gin or vodka
1 ounce maple syrup
lemon juice to taste

Fill a cocktail shaker with ice and pour in gin or vodka. Add maple syrup and lemon juice. (The juice cuts the sweetness and viscosity of the heavier syrup.) Shake until well mixed and cold. Pour into a chilled cocktail glass.

Angostura Shots

Angostura bitters were a legal substitute for liquor, helpful for stomach ailments and used throughout the UP. Nelsen's Bitter Hall on Washington Island just south of the UP border serves this specialty beverage.

1½ ounces angostura bitters
glass of water or soft drink to wash it down

Fill shot glass with bitters. Finish with water or soft drink of choice.

Brandied Cherries

Italians brought brandied cherries to the Upper Peninsula. They were popular as a "snack-shot" when men were visiting. They were consumed in small amounts. Cherries were obtained during the summer when available. The cherries were washed in water, and the stems were cut down but not removed, as they had to be intact to allow the alcohol to gradually enter the fruit without making it soggy.

8- to 10-ounce jelly jar
cherries, enough to fill jar
4 to 5 ounces liquor of choice

Place the fruit in a glass jar, the size depending on how large a quantity you want to make. Usually, a small jelly jar is used. Fill with the cherries; then add whiskey, brandy or any other liquor you want to the rim so that the fruit is immersed. Tightly cap the bottle and place in a cool spot. Cherries bottled in July are ready for serving by late December and are usually given as presents for the holidays. The snack-shot should be carefully consumed, as the fruit meat is filled with liquor.

CANADIAN GRENADIER

UP residents living close to the Canadian border could easily travel to Sault Ste. Marie, Ontario, after 1927 and enjoy their drinks without the prospect of a police raid.

1 ounce gin
Canadian Dry Ginger Ale

Add gin to a cocktail shaker filled with ice. Shake well and strain into chilled highball glass. Top with ginger ale and serve with a straw.

COFFEE ROYAL

The coffee royal was popular with many people but especially with Italian immigrants even before Prohibition. With the coming of Prohibition, the coffee could help mask the aroma of the brandy or whiskey. In some cases, it would be consumed as a breakfast drink or to warm you up on a cold winter night.

1 cup strong, hot coffee
1 ounce whiskey or brandy
lemon peel
sugar to taste

Fill a cup with coffee. Pour in whiskey or brandy. Cut a sliver of lemon peel and twist, adding it to the coffee. You are ready to keep warm.

COFFEE CHATHAM

A variation on the coffee royal that was popular with rural people in the farming area around Chatham, populated by Finns and Finnish lumberjacks. Its Prohibition ingredient was lemon extract, which could have an alcohol content of 95 percent. It is presented here to give the reader an idea of a down-to-earth drink made without moonshine.

1 cup strong hot coffee
⅛ ounce lemon extract
sugar

Pour the coffee into a cup and add lemon extract and sugar to taste. Be careful with the extract, as it is strong under any conditions.

Highland Fling

This was a drink born of Prohibition and is based on moonshine. It first appeared in John Voelker's Danny and the Boys *and was popular in the hunting camps and haunts of the Ishpeming area. Probably during the era, lemon juice was replaced with some lemon extract, which added an extra "kick" to the drink.*

3 ounces moonshine, gin or vodka
dash lemon juice
sugar
boiling water

Place moonshine, gin or vodka in a cup. Add lemon juice and sugar to taste and mix well. Add boiling water to the cup. Adjust ingredients to taste.

Lime Rickey

A refreshing summer drink, the Lime Rickey was found in many resorts around the eastern Upper Peninsula.

½ a lime
1 teaspoon sugar syrup
1 ounce gin
seltzer

Crush lime in highball glass and add syrup and cracked ice. Stir in gin, and add seltzer to fill. Serve with straws.

Menthe

For everyone who tried to rid himself or herself of the taste of bad UP moonshine, the addition of crème de menthe was an immediate treat. Such simple drinks were often available to travelers at gas stations, much as soft drinks are today, or at speakeasies.

½ ounce crème de menthe
½ ounce gin

Place crème de menthe and gin in a cocktail shaker and shake well with ice; strain into a chilled cocktail glass or paper cup and serve.

MILK HIGHBALL

"Shorty" Perron's Restaurant was located in the notorious Midway of Iron Mountain, where wine, women and song dominated the scene. In an effort to return the area to normal, Chief of Police Rudolph Freeman and prosecutor Ray McAllister decided to raid the dives. Two of their investigators entered Perron's and ordered coffee or tea, which Shorty did not have. He did have milk, which he provided for them and asked if they wanted "a little shot" in the milk? Thus, a new drink was born in the spring of 1926.

8 ounces cold milk
1 to 2 ounces whiskey or gin

Fill a glass with milk and add the liquor for a unique taste.

OLD FASHIONED

John Voelker (aka Robert Traver) was a leading Upper Peninsula author from Ishpeming, best known for his novel Anatomy of the Murder. *His signature drink, the Old Fashioned, dates from Prohibition and remains a popular drink in Ishpeming taverns and clubs to the present day.*

Here is the recipe as given by John's good friend Ted Bogdan, who saw it made and enjoyed countless times, especially at fishing camp.

> *John would start by pouring a little water in an old fashioned glass. He would macerate one cube of sugar. Add ice. Then he would provide the booze… originally Cabin Still bourbon but later Jim Beam—2 shots; squeeze an orange and add maraschino cherries and a couple of drops of angostura bitters and you have the John Voelker version of the Old Fashioned.*

SHOT & BEER

A simple recipe that included several shots of whiskey, this was served in speakeasies to miners or lumberjacks when they came from work.

1 to 2 ounces whiskey
16 ounces beer

Pour the whiskey in a standard shot glass and the beer in a pint glass. Alternate drinking the two beverages. Repeat as desired.

Vocabulary of Prohibition

The bulk of the following terms were found in Upper Peninsula newspapers and date from the 1920s, during the height of Prohibition.

apply the sponge: after an arrest, padlock the site for a year.

bathtub gin: from 1930, a homemade spirit concocted from raw alcohol, water, essences and essential oils.

beer flat: second-floor speakeasy where beer was sold.

blind pig: see blind tiger.

blind tiger: term dates from 1857 and refers to a place that sells illegal intoxicants.

dry navy: land-based police that was the alcohol enforcement along rivers.

dry squad: federal enforcement agents.

gingerie: Prohibition drink made with Jamaican ginger mixed in water.

grape brick: California wine grapes that were concentrated, dried and legally sold and shipped with instructions on how not to turn it into wine.

jake: a popular name for Jamaican ginger, a medicinal substitute for alcohol.

liquor fishing: to "fish" for liquor that had gone through ice during the winter.

masher: the fellow who maintained the mash supply in a still operation.

moonlight: an early but little-used term replaced by moonshine.

moonshine: illegally distilled corn whiskey whose quality was questioned.

moonshine plants: locations where stills were set up, usually referring to large complexes.

on the hip: liquor flask in the hip pocket.

order of booze dispensers: newspaper terms for bootleggers.

play the game: term used by federal agents when they had to act to enter speakeasy and gain evidence.

primed: underage youths' consumption of liquor to be fortified before a dance.

raisin wine: wine made from raisins, which at times replaced grapes, that could be distilled.

rum hound: Michigan state police

rumrunning: illegal business of transporting (smuggling) alcoholic beverages where they are illegal by law.

smart: underage youths' acquisition of liquor for consumption before a dance.

society bootlegger: one who caters to the upper strata of the trade.

soda pop: Midwest term for carbonated beverage.

speakeasy: dating from 1889, the term became common during Prohibition as a place where alcoholic beverages are illegally sold.

sponge detective: federal enforcement agent.

sponge squad: federal enforcement agents.

spotter: bootlegger agents who watched for federal agents or police.

sure death: moonshine from an unknown source that could be poisonous and deadly.

tanglefoot: moonshine of an unknown distiller that could be deadly.

wet spots: places where liquor was sold or found.

white mule: clear moonshine with a "kick" and wallop.

white mule traffic: moonshine trade.

white stuff: another term for white mule or moonshine.

Bibliography

Allen, Frederick Lewis. *Only Yesterday: An Informal History of the Nineteen Twenties*. New York: Harper & Bros., 1931.

———. *Since Yesterday: The Nineteen Thirties in America*. New York: Harper & Row, 1940.

Alperovitz, David. Interview. Digital Collection Bay College Library, Escanaba, MI.

Andra-Warner, Elle. "Bootleg Booze and Gangster Al Capone," *Northernwilds* 11, no. 4 (May 2014): 14.

Atwood, Stephanie, and Katrina Vestal. "Ways to Get Through the Night: Crimes in the Early Post-Copper Boom Keweenaw." *Superior Signal* 14, no. 3 (August 1999): 12–13.

Bachus, Rich. "In the 1920s Gambling Rolled in Harbor Springs." *Traverse City Record Eagle*, November 5, 1995.

Bacon, Betty Byrnes. *Lighthouse Memories: Growing Up at Point Iroquois in the 1920s*. Brimley, MI: Bay Mills–Brimley Historical Research Society, 1989.

Barr, Andrew. *Drink: A Social History of America*. New York: Carroll & Graf Publishers, 1999.

Behr, Edward. *Prohibition: Thirteen Years That Changed America*. New York: Arcade Publishing, 2011.

Benzoni, Peter. *Beyond the Mine: A Steelworker's Story*. Superior, WI: Savage Press, 1997.

Betts, Blaine. Interview. Marquette, Michigan, September 1, 2015, deposited with the Central Upper Peninsula and University Archives, Northern Michigan University, Marquette, MI.

Bingham, Abel. "The Early Mission at Sault Ste. Marie." *Michigan Pioneer and Historical Collection* 28 (1897–98): 520–24.

Black, Rachel, ed. *Alcohol in Popular Culture: An Encyclopedia*. Santa Barbara, CA: Greenwood Publishing Group, 2010.

Blumenthal, Karen. *Bootleg, Murder, Moonshine and the Lawless Years of Prohibition*. New York: Roaring Brook Press, 2014.

Boothby, "Cocktail Bill." *World Drinks and How to Mix Them*. Rev. ed., 1934. San Francisco, CA: Boothby World Drinks Company, 1930.

Brown, John H. *Early American Beverages*. New York: Bonanza Books, 1966.

Butts, Edward. *Outlaws of the Lakes: Bootlegging and Smuggling from Colonial Times to Prohibition*. Toronto, ON: Lynx Images Inc., 2004.

Canney, Donald L. *U.S. Coast Guard and Revenue Cutters, 1790–1935*. Annapolis, MD: Naval Institute Press, 1995.

Chabot, Larry. "Prohibition-Era Gangsters Weren't Strangers to the U.P." *Marquette Monthly* (June 2012).

Clock, Robert. "Club Manitou Opened Up as the Stork Club of the North." *Petoskey News Review*, March 19, 1969.

———. "An Era Ends with Death of the Harbor Springs Club Owner." *Petoskey News Review*, December 17, 1987.

Crutchfield, James A., Robin Hood and Randall K. Powers. *Grand Hotel: America's Summer Place*. Franklin, TN: Grandin Hood Publishers, 2012.

Devlin, Shelia F. "Working with Water, Goulais Mission Memories." *Canadian Journal of Native Studies* 22, no. 2 (2002): 269–86.

Duchaine, William J. "Yo Ho, Ho, How the Swabs Made Way for Roaring Dan, The Lone Pirate of Lake Michigan." *Chicago Tribune*, April 22, 1962.

Engelmann, Larry. *Intemperance: The Lost War Against Liquor*. New York: Free Press, 1979.

———. "The Iron River Rum Rebellion." *Mid-America* 55 (January 1973): 37–53.

Eustice, Sally. *History from the Hearth: A Colonial Michilimackinac Cookbook*. Mackinac Island, MI: Mackinac State Historic Parks, 1997.

Farley, Amanda. Interview. Digital Collection from Bay College Library, Escanaba, MI.

Fisher, Claude. Interview. Digital Collection Bay College Library, Escanaba, MI.

Fortune Editor. "United States Liquor Industry." *Fortune Magazine* 4, no. 4 (October 1931): 53–56, 118, 120.

Fundenburg, J. Anne. *Bootleggers and Beer Barons of the Prohibition Era*. Jefferson, NC: McFarland & Company, 2014.

Gianunzio, Fiore. *Mangia Ferro! "The Iron Eater": The Story of a Rugged Italian Immigrant and His Family in the 20th Century*. Iron Mountain, MI: Piers Gorge Press, 1999.

Gore, Russell. "State Police in U.P. Are Lauded for Their Many Brave Actions." *Ironwood Daily Globe*, December 9, 1925.

Grossman, Ron. "Just Listed: Only $12 Million." *Chicago Tribune*, August 2, 1990.

Hallowell, Gerald A. "Prohibition in Ontario." Master's thesis, Carleton University, 1966.

Helman, Lou Ellyn, and Maria Vezzetti Matson. *Gelsomina's Story of Cesar Lucchesi: A True Tale of Italian Immigrants*. San Francisco, CA: Polenta Publishing Co., 2011.

Hemingway, Ernest. "Rum-Running: Canuck Whiskey Pouring into the U.S." *Toronto Star Weekly*, June 5, 1920. Reprinted: *Dateline: Toronto; The Complete Toronto Star Dispatches, 1920–1924*. New York: Simon & Schuster, 2002: 54–56.

Hobart, Henry. *Copper Country Journal: The Diary of Schoolmaster Henry Hobart, 1863–1864*. Edited by Philip P. Mason. Detroit, MI: Wayne State University Press, 1991.

Hrebec, Jessica, and Mandy Hattala. "Prohibition: The Keweenaw's Defiance of a Failing Amendment." *Superior Signal* 16, no. 1 (February 2001): 20–22.

Hummasti, P.G. "'Hyvä Toivo' The Finnish-American Temperance Movement." *Journal of Finnish Studies* 13, no. 1 (Summer 2009): 48–57.

Joyce, Jaime. *A Cultural History of America's Infamous Liquor*. Minneapolis, MN: Zenith Press, 2014.

Kalm, Peter. "The Method for Making Spruce Beer as Practiced in North America, from the letters of P. Kalm sent to the Swedish Academy." *Gentleman's Magazine and Historical Chronicle* 22 (September 1752): 399–400.

———. *Travels in North America*. Edited by Adolph B. Benson. New York: Dover Publications, 1987.

Kegerreis, Sharon, and Lorri Hathaway. *The History of Michigan Wines: 150 Year of Winemaking Along the Great Lakes*. Charleston, SC: The History Press, 2010.

———. "Wine Rebellion in Northern Michigan's Upper Peninsula." *Traverse Magazine*, January 5, 2011.

Kohl, Johann Georg. *Kitchi-Gami: Life Among the Lake Superior Ojibway*. Translated by Lascelles Wraxall. St. Paul: Minnesota Historical Society Press, 1985.

Kowalski, Greg. *Prohibition in Hamtranck, Gangsters, Gunfights & Getaways*. Charleston, SC: The History Press, 2015.

Kyvig, David E. *Repealing National Prohibition*. Chicago: University of Chicago Press, 1979. Second edition: Kent, OH: Kent State University Press, 2000.

Lämpää, Elmer, and Eddy Jääkkälä. "Viina Trokarin Laulu (Bootleggers Song)." Chicago: Victor Records (80072), 1927.

Lämpää, Elmer, and H. Saarinen. "Pelti Liisa (Tin Lizzie)." Camden, NJ: Victor Records (80467), 1927.

———. "Poliisina Ollessani (Policeman's Song)." Camden, NJ: Victor Records (80759), circa 1928.

Lankton, Larry. *Beyond the Boundaries: Life and Landscape at the Lake Superior Copper Mines, 1840–1875*. New York: Oxford University Press, 1997.

Lefebvre, Andrew. "Prohibition and the Smuggling of Intoxicating Liquors Between the Two Saults." *Northern Mariner/Le marin du nord* 11, no. 3 (July 2001): 33–40.

Magnaghi, Grace. *Grace and Mario's Honeymoon Trip, August 1931*. Edited by Russell M. Magnaghi. Marquette, MI: 906 Heritage, 2015.

Magnaghi, Russell M. *Beer in the Upper Peninsula: History of Brewing Above the Bridge*. Charleston, SC: The History Press, 2015.

Martenhoff, Jim. "Speedboat King: Gar Wood." *Motor Boating*, July 1964: 62, 97–98.

Mason, Philip P. "Anyone Who Couldn't Get a Drink Wasn't Trying: Rumrunning Along the Michigan-Ontario Border During Prohibition." *Michigan History* 78 (1994): 12–22.

———. *Rum Running and the Roaring Twenties: Prohibition on the Michigan-Ontario Waterway*. Detroit, MI: Wayne State University Press, 1995.

McCabe, John. *Grand Hotel, Mackinac Island*. Sault Ste. Marie, MI: Unicorn Press, 1987.

McQuarrie, Willis John. *Whisky Smugglers of the North Channel*. Gore Bay, ON: Mid-North Printers & Publishers, 2003.

Mercer, Gerg. "When Bootlegging Reigned, Bullets Flew over Waterloo." *Waterloo Regional Record*, December 19, 2014.

Milwaukee Journal. "Only 48 Stores Operating Now." April 1, 1934.

Monette, Clarence J. *Joseph Bosch and the Bosch Brewing Company*. Lake Linden, MI: Privately published, 1978.

Morison, Daniel. *The Doctor's Secret Journal: A True Account of Violence at Fort Michilimackinac*. Edited by George S. May. Mackinac Island, MI: Mackinac State Historic Parks, 1960.

Mount, Graeme S., John Abbott and Michael J. Mulloy. *The Border at Sault Ste. Marie*. Toronto, ON: Dundurn Press, 1995.

Newman, Peter C. *King of the Castle, The Making of a Dynasty: Seagram's and the Bronfman Empire*. New York: Antheneum, 1979.

Noble, Dennis. *Great Lakes: A Brief History of the United States Coast Guard Operations*. Washington, D.C.: Commandant's Bulletin Bicentennial Series, 1990.

O'Dell, Richard, and Richard Sonderegger. "North of Sahara: Marquette in the Dry Decade." Unpublished paper, Marquette Regional History Center, J.M. Longyear Research Library, 1971.

Okrent, Daniel. *Last Call: The Rise and Fall of Prohibition*. New York: Scribner's, 2011.

Ostrom, Thomas P., and John J. Galluzzo. *United States Coast Guard Leaders and Missions, 1790 to the Present*. Jefferson, NC: McFarland, 2015.

Payne, A.W. "Twenty Million Dollars Planned for Motor Boats." *Motor Boating* 33:1 (January 1924): 80.

Pegram, Thomas R. *One Hundred Percent American: The Rebirth and Decline of the Ku Klux Klan in the 1920s*. Chicago: Ivan R. Dee, 2011.

Pekkärinen, Tätu, and Mätti Jurvä. "Vänhat Viinaveikot (Wine Drinking Buddies)." New York: Victor Records (8631), 1928.

Peters, Bernard C. "The Impact of Alcohol on the Indians of the Great Lakes/Upper Mississippi Region: Some First Hand Accounts of the 'Drunken Frolic,'" in *Northern Border. History and Lore of Michigan's Upper Peninsula and Beyond in Honor of Russell Magnaghi*. Edited by Robert Archibald. Marquette: Northern Michigan University Press, 2014, 168–89.

Peters, Scott M. *Making Waves: Michigan's Boat Building Industry, 1865–2000*. Ann Arbor: University of Michigan Press, 2015.

Phare, Cory, ed., et al. *Backyards of Gwinn*. Gwinn, MI: Privately published, 1995.

Rauch, William. "Recalling Harbor Springs in the Era of Prohibition and Gambling." *Harbor Light News*, November 1981.

———. "Recalling Harbor Springs in the Era of Prohibition and Gambling." *Traverse City Record Eagle*, November 5, 1995.

RAW. "Repeals by Implication: Prohibition in Michigan." *Michigan Law Review* 17, no. 6 (April 1919): 495–597.

Reimann, Lewis C. *Between the Iron and the Pine*. Ann Arbor, MI: Northwoods Publishers, 1951.

———. *Hurley: Still No Angel*. Ann Arbor, MI: Northwoods Publishers, 1954.

Superior Signal, "Remember Buffalos?" August 1990: 10–11.

Report on the Enforcement of the Prohibition Laws of the United States National Commission on Law Observance and Enforcement (The Wickersham Commission Report on Alcohol Prohibition). Dated January 7, 1931.

Rodengen, Jeffery I. *The Legend of Chris-Craft*. 3rd edition. Fort Lauderdale, FL: Write Stuff Syndicate, 1998.

Rorbaugh, W.J. *The Alcoholic Republic: An American Tradition*. New York: Oxford University Press, 1979.

Ross, C. *The Finn Factor in American Labor, Culture, and Society*. New York Mills, MN: Parta Printers, 1977.

Sariola, S. "The Finnish Temperance Movement in the Great Lakes Area of the Midwest," *Contemporary Drug Problems* 12 (1985): 287–307.

Schertzing, Philip D. *Preserve, Protect, and Defend: An Illustrated History of the Michigan State Police in the 20th Century*. Puducah, KY: Turner Publishing Co., 2002.

Schwartz, James Z. "Taming the 'Savagery' of Michigan's Indians." *Michigan Historical Review* 34, no. 2 (Fall 2008): 39–56.

Scott, S.J., and Martin J. Scott. "Catholics and the Ku Klux Klan." *North American Review* 223 (June 1926): 272, 274.

Sedlock, George. "Michigan and Alcohol Have Sordid Past." *Marquette Monthly*, May 2009.

Smith, E. Ann. "Drinking Practices and Glassware of the British Military, circa 1755–85." *Northeast Historical Archaeology* 12 (1983): 31–39.

Spivak, Mark. *Moonshine Nation: The Art of Creating Cornbread in a Bottle*. Guilford, CT: Globe Pequot, 2014.

Straus, Frank. "Prohibition's 'International Trade' Helped Pay Fenlon's Tuition." *(Mackinac Island) Town Crier*, December 11, 2010.

Stonehouse, Frederick. *Great Lakes Crime: Murder, Mayhem, Booze & Broads*. Gwinn, MI: Avery Color Studios Inc., 2004.

———. *Great Lakes Crime II: Murder, Mayhem, Booze & Broads*. Gwinn, MI: Avery Color Studios Inc., 2007.

———. *Pirates, Crooks & Killers: The Dark Side of the Great Lakes*. Gwinn, MI: Avery Color Studios Inc., 2013.

Sturgul, Paul A. "History of Hurley, Frontier Phase—1880s to 1920." Presented at the Sonderegger Symposium 15, September 11, 2015. Northern Michigan University, Marquette, MI.

Sulkunen, I. *History of the Finnish Temperance Movement: Temperance as a Civic Religion*. Translated by M. Hall. Lewiston, NY: Edwin Mellen Press, 1990.

Sullivan, Patrick. "Booze Flowed Freely through Northern Michigan during Prohibition." *Northern Express Weekly*, May 25, 2015, 12–13.

Supanich, Nancy. "Prohibition Didn't Leave Baraga County Dry." *Mining Journal*, May 20, 1990.

Thwaites, Reuben G., ed. *The Jesuit Relations and Allied Documents*. 73 vols. New York: Pageant Book Co., 1959.

Traver, Robert. *Danny and the Boys, Being Some Legends of Hungry Hollow*. 1951; reprint, Detroit: Wayne State University Press, 1987.

Trout Lake Women's Club. *Tales and Trails of Tro-La-Oz-Ken*. Trout Lake, MI: Trout Lake Women's Club, 1976.

United States National Archives and Records Administration. Record Group 59, Consular Correspondence of the American Consulate at Fort William (1915–1948), Port Arthur (1915–1948) and Sault Ste. Marie, Ontario (1906–1937).

Waters, Harold. *Smugglers and Spirits: Prohibition and the Coast Guard Patrol*. New York: Hastings House 1971.

Wiles, Richard. "The Infamous Club Manitou." *Mackinac Journal*, December 2013.

Willoughby, Malcolm. *Rum Row*. New York: Rinehart & Co., 1959.

Wood, Ike. *One Hundred Years at Hard Labor, A History of Marquette Prison*. Marquette, MI: Privately printed, 1985.

Worth, Jean. "Prohibition Era Ended 30 Years Ago." *Escanaba Daily Press*, December 2, 1963.

Zeitz, Joshua. *Flapper: A Madcap Story of Sex, Style, Celebrity, and the Women Who Made Modern America*. New York: Broadway Books, 2007.

Index

E

F

G

H

I

J

K

L

M

N

O

P

About the Author

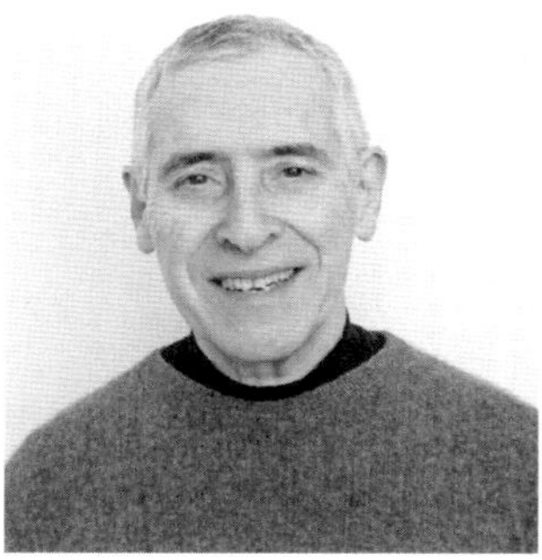

Russsell Magnaghi, noted and award-winning historian of Michigan's Upper Peninsula, has had a four-decade-long interest in the food and beverage of the region. However, his origins go back to San Francisco, California, where his family assisted people enjoying coffee royals, home-brewed beer and dago red. In the UP, he has pursued the study of Prohibition and interviewed dozens of old-timers who followed a similar tradition, violating the Eighteenth Amendment. He enjoys a fine martini and local craft beers and is the author of over a dozen books on the UP, the most recent, *Upper Peninsula Beer: A History of Brewing Above the Bridge*. Recently, he developed a tiny hop yard and had a batch of beer made from it. A graduate of the University of San Francisco and St. Louis University, he taught for forty-five years at Northern Michigan University. He and his wife, Diane, reside in Marquette and Traverse City.